Killer whale in full breach

SEASONS *on the*
PACIFIC COAST

A Naturalist's Notebook

BY SUSAN J. TWEIT

Illustrations by James Noel Smith

CHRONICLE BOOKS
SAN FRANCISCO

Library of Congress Cataloging-in-
Publication Data:

Tweit, Susan J.
    Seasons on the Pacific Coast : a
naturalist's notebook / by Susan J.
Tweit ; illustrations by James Noel
Smith.
        p. cm.
    Includes bibliographical
    references.
ISBN 0-8118-2080-7
1. Coastal animals—Pacific Coast
(North America) 2. Coastal plants—
Pacific Coast (North America) 3.
Seasons—Pacific Coast (North
America) I. Title.
QL151.T94 1999
578.769'9'0979—dc21   98-31312
                        CIP

Printed in Hong Kong.

Design by Shawn Hazen

Distributed in Canada by
Raincoast Books
8680 Cambie Street
Vancouver, British Columbia
V6P 6M9

10 9 8 7 6 5 4 3 2 1

Chronicle Books
85 Second Street
San Francisco, California 94105

www.chroniclebooks.com

For my brother, Bill Tweit, who carries the ocean in his blood; my nieces, Heather, Anna, Sienna, and Alice Joan, born within sight of Puget Sound; my sister-in-law, Lucy Winter, who may yet evolve webbed feet; and my daughter, Molly Cabe, making a home in the land of slugs.

And for Karen Silver, an artist among editors, who inspired this book.

Acknowledgments

WRITING ABOUT A REGION FROM AFAR is never easy. Thanks to all who answered my questions, read my essays, and referred me to sources of information. In particular, thanks to Bob Carr, Adventure Kayaks; John DeVore, Washington State Department of Fisheries and Wildlife; Mia Monroe, U.S. National Park Service; Craig Partridge, Washington State Department of Natural Resources; Robert Michael Pyle, author and entomologist; Robert C. and Joan C. Tweit; and the staff at the Monterey Bay Aquarium. And thanks to my lifeline to the larger world of information, the staff at the Salida Regional Library, especially Brenda Wiard and Becky Nelson.

To Clifford Burke and Alison Deming, thanks for the inspiration of your poetry. I am humbled by your ability to tell stories with such economy and beauty. Thanks also to Jennifer McDonald, the best combination of agent, mentor, and friend I could ask for.

The staff at Chronicle Books is wonderful to work with. Special thanks to my editor, Jay Schaefer, for taking me on; to Kate Chynoweth and Steve Mockus, his assistants; to copy editor Lisa Zuniga; and to managing publicist Sarah McFall Bailey. These stories are for you all.

To James Noel Smith, for portraying in the illustrations what I've tried to say in words. It's as if you read my mind—and you have a sense of humor, as well! Thank you, James.

A writer's life can be such a solitary one, because we spend so much time spinning stories to ourselves. I am fortunate in having a supportive and thoughtful community of friends and colleagues near and far. Thanks especially to those on the Pacific coast—Marlene Blessing, Linda Kunze, Don Norman, Lisa Dale Norton, Craig Partridge, Mary Ransome, Bob Rose, Blanche Sobottke, and Terry Winfield. For company on various expeditions to the coast, thanks to my parents (who have even learned to tolerate my dog), Blanche Sobottke ("Road-Trip Queen"), and most of all to my family, Molly and Richard Cabe, the best of companions, and our dog, Perdida Imelda. Thanks as well to fellow writers Denise Chávez, Michael Evans-Smith, Verne Huser, Anne-Marie Mackler, John Murray, Gary Paul Nabhan, and Linda Peterson for encouragement and friendship. And to my neighbor Beverly Gray, thanks for being there when I'm not, as well as when I am.

I couldn't write without the encouragement and support of my family, especially my husband, Richard, the love of my life, and Molly, as wonderful a daughter as anybody could ever ask for. Thanks as well to my parents for their help in so many ways, to my brother, Bill, my sister-in-law, Lucy, and my nieces—Heather and her husband, Duane, Sienna, and Alice. I love you all! This book is also for my "other" family—Cabe, Hitz, and Gifford—especially the Puget Sound Cabes and Mortons, and Jennifer Cabe and Paul Childress in Portland.

Finally, a much belated thanks to three guys who shaped my understanding of the way the natural world works and taught me to think for myself (I hope you're not sorry!): John Richardson, Phil Robertson, and John Yopp at Southern Illinois University in Carbondale.

Any errors, misinterpretations, or omissions are—of course—my own responsibility.

Table of Contents

Introduction 10

SPRING 15

17 Eelgrass
22 Rough-skinned Newt
27 California Poppy
31 Black Oystercatcher
35 Giant Pacific Octopus
40 California Grunion
44 Red Abalone
49 Blueblossom
54 Pacific Madrone
59 White Sturgeon

SUMMER 64

66 Southern Sea Otter
71 Cabezon
76 Cobra Lily
80 Xerces Blue Butterfly
85 Bat Ray
89 Light-footed Clapper Rail
94 Orca
99 Geoduck Clam
103 Giant Green Anemone
108 Marbled Murrelet

FALL 113

115 Harford's Greedy Isopod
119 California Least Tern
124 Eccentric Sand Dollar
129 Pickleweed
134 Giant Acorn Barnacle
139 Brown Pelican
144 Diatoms
149 Moon Jellyfish
154 Harbor Seal
159 Chum Salmon

WINTER 165

167 Giant Bladder Kelp
172 Sanderling
177 Spanish Shawl
182 Island Fox
187 Monarch Butterfly
192 Gray Whale
197 Western Gull
201 Banana Slug
206 Coast Redwood

Recommended Readings & Places to Visit 212

Introduction

If there is poetry in my book about the sea, it is not because I deliberately put it there, but because no one could write truthfully about the sea and leave out the poetry.

—Rachel Carson,
accepting the National Book Award
for *The Sea Around Us,* 1952

THERE ARE AS MANY DEFINITIONS of the Pacific Coast region as there are people to define it. This book treats the two-thousand-mile stretch of the Pacific coast that I know best, from Vancouver Island, British Columbia, to Tijuana, Mexico. Water tells the story of this narrow belt where ocean meets land and fog blankets the landscape at least part of the year. Seawater physically shapes the landscape as surely as the waves crash against the shore. Water—either salt or fresh—clothes it with life, and the distribution of water—as rain or fog—separates this edge into regions as distinct as subcontinents.

From Vancouver Island, where 150 inches of rain—that's 12.5 *feet* of water—may fall in a year, to Tijuana, where one-tenth of that, or 15 inches a year, is a luxury, the character of the coast changes dramatically. Up north, where moisture is plentiful, the landscape is buried under a thick, wet growth of temperate rain forest, a jungle of sorts. Summer, residents of this part of the region joke, comes one weekend in July or August between rains. Down south, in southern California and northern Baja California, summer sticks around for much of the year, and rain falls in abundance only in winter. From April to November, the ocean gives none of its moisture to the land. With drought for half the year, the vegetation is tough and desertlike, forming a shrubby chaparral at the lower elevations as aromatic as it is flammable. Moisture is only abundant here in winter, and then it is sometimes too abundant, falling in torrents that fill up normally dry arroyos, lubricate unstable slopes, and send mudslides and buildings alike tumbling downhill.

With all its diversity, one characteristic unites this region: the presence of the ocean. No matter where you are along the coast, in the dripping northern forests or the dry southern chaparral, even in the concrete heart of the region's busiest cities, the sea constantly makes itself known, whether as subtly as a breeze bearing the sound of crying seagulls and the odors of salt and drying algae or as blatantly as the blanket of fog creeping inland at night. From sun-drenched San Diego and Tijuana to rain-drenched Seattle and Vancouver, the damp, clammy presence of fog at least part of the year draws a distinct, if watery, line between the coastal climate and the much drier terrestrial climate inland. Within this fog belt, it is as if the ocean periodically reimmerses the land, blanketing it in a gray veil of water droplets diffused in the air. Up and down the coast, fog shapes the vegetation on land, its fine beading of moisture nurturing redwood groves in narrow canyons, moss-carpeted rain forests, and gray strands of fog-sipping lichen that drape the limbs of coastal pines and cypresses.

Edges are magical places, diverse and full of possibility. The edge where land meets sea along the Pacific coast is no exception. Unlike the largely low Atlantic coast, with its profusion of sheltered bays, estuaries, and inlets, the Pacific coast is by and large a cliff edge studded with headlands, points, and capes, and boasting only a handful of natural harbors along its wave-battered margin.

The rugged character of the Pacific coast is due largely to the geological edge that shapes the coastline. Deep under the earth's crust, slow movements in the semiliquid rocks of the mantle drag the solid crustal plates around the way the liquid lava in an active flow drags along the hardened material at the flow's surface. At the coast, two slow-moving crustal plates meet and collide: the expanding Pacific Ocean plate, headed roughly northeast, grinds against the western edge of the continental plate. The heavier rocks of the oceanic plate crumple, sink, and partially melt under the less dense rocks of the continent. The continual pressure of one plate grinding against the other causes the earthquakes and tremors felt up and down the coast. It also creates the Coast Ranges, chunks of crust crashed at odd angles along the coast like huge twisted and crumpled car wrecks, and the conical peaks of the northern coast's still active volcanoes.

The Pacific Coast is an ecological edge as well, where lives adapted to terrestrial existence meet lives adapted to saltwater immersion. As terrestrial beings, we see this edge from the perspective of our (normally) land-bound bodies: standing on land, bathed in the air we breathe, we look into the foreign world of the ocean. From the perspective of a sponge, held fast to a rock on the bottom, or a passing whale, the edge looks different: dry land is the foreign place, impossibly arid and glaring in the harsh sunlight. The boundary between ecosystems is as abrupt as the physical coastline itself: few lives can exist in both the aquatic and the terrestrial world.

Although as abrupt as the change from air to water, the ocean's tides blur the exact line between the two ecosystems, moving the ocean's edge up and down the shore. Tides are a testament to the force of gravity exerted by nearby planets. As the earth turns on its axis and orbits the sun, the gravitational fields of the moon and sun pull the water in the oceans from one shore to the other. Each lunar day (not quite twenty-four hours) has two high tides, or flood tides, and two low tides, or ebb tides. The most extreme tides occur when the sun, moon, and earth are in line, as they are just after a full moon and a new moon. During these "spring" tides, the combined gravitational pull of the sun and moon causes higher high tides and lower low tides. (*Spring*, from the Anglo-Saxon *sprungen*, "a strong action," in this case refers to upwelling rather than to the season.) However, both the moon and sun's orbits are elliptical. Twice a month, the moon reaches the point on its orbit when it is closest to earth. If this coincides with high tide, the tide will be 40 percent higher, the low tide correspondingly lower. The sun reaches its closest point to the earth in June and December. High and low tides of these months are thus the most extreme of the year. When the moon is in its quarter phases, it is at right angles to, and partially counteracts, the pull of the sun. The tidal movements in these times are slack, neither particularly high nor particularly low. These sluggish tides are called "neap" tides, from a Scandinavian root for "barely touching."

As the tides advance and retreat, alternately immersing and baring the shoreline, life responds accordingly. When the tide is in, an abundance of lives flourish in the temporary ocean: barnacles, sea worms, mussels, sea anemones, and other more or less immobile creatures extend their feeding appendages to trap food brought by the sea; snails, starfish, crabs, and other bottom-feeders move about, grazing or on the hunt; and fish and rays swim toward the shore to feed. As the water draws away, exposing the shore to the air, barnacles, mussels, and other shelled animals slam their doors shut; sea worms take shelter in their burrows and sea anemones go limp; snails close their operculums; starfish and crabs retreat to the damp undersides of rocks; fish and rays move back out to sea. This interplay between ocean and land, and between freshwater and salt where streams and rivers meet the ocean, is what makes the coast such a complex and fascinating ecological edge, a zone where dramatically different environments overlap.

I am a tourist on this shore. Although I lived near Puget Sound for three wet years, and visited my mother's family in the San Francisco Bay Area throughout my childhood, the coast has never been my home. Still, I cannot resist its pull, as if I, too, respond to the tides. Hence this book, which grew out of my fascination with the edge where land and sea blur, not quite separate, but not merged either. It is my homage to a region that is foreign yet somehow familiar, like tales of kin from exotic cultures. I chose the particular plants and animals profiled here—out of thousands of possibilities—because their stories reflect the coast's vibrant and magical diversity. They may represent some extraordinary adaptation to coastal life, or a crucial relationship; they may be characteristic of a particular environment, or they may be included simply because their life story intrigues me.

The profiles are grouped by season, depending on what time of year each animal or plant is most prominent or on some seasonal event in the story of its life. Each opens with the common name or names of the plant or animal, its scientific name, and a quote relating to the subject. Following the quote is a paragraph giving the facts about the creature or plant's life: where it lives, what its names mean, how big it is, its color, and other details. Then comes the "family story," a personal essay about that particular coastal life and how I know it. At the back of the book is "Recommended Readings & Places to Visit," a section giving tips on where to learn more about a particular plant or animal and suggestions on where or how to see it.

I hope you will read this book as you would a family album, with affection, interest, and a renewed sense of the kinship we have with all life. The characters profiled here are our relatives, fellow creatures whose lives affect our own whether we are aware of it or not. Collectively, through their interactions with each other and with the environment, they make the Pacific Coast the unique and awesome place it is. May the stories of these wild relatives rekindle your connection to the coastal world.

S P R I N G

SPRING COMES IN WET along the entire Pacific Coast, but the moisture doesn't last in the southern part of the region. With the lengthening days comes a change in the storm pattern from central California south, beginning the yearly drought. From April until November, rain is a rare occurrence on this part of the coast, although fog banks may coalesce just offshore. The season of spring here is warm, sunny, and dry, just right for tanning, surfing, sailing, and other traditional southern California pursuits. Farther north, however, spring generally remains chill and wet, more conducive to nurturing ducks and slugs than humans.

Despite the wide variation in weather, spring means migratory birds and spectacular wildflower displays both up and down the coast. Clouds of shorebirds and waterfowl wing up the coast in spring, headed for nesting grounds in the far north. One of the most easily accessible places to see awesome numbers of migratory shore- and waterbirds is San Francisco Bay National Wildlife Refuge. In late March and early April one *million* birds pass through these urban marshes each day, estimates the U.S. Fish and Wildlife Service, feeding and resting within view of hundreds of thousands of human commuters. From mid-April to early May, the flocks of shorebirds are equally impressive at Bowerman Basin in Grays Harbor National Wildlife Refuge near Hoquiam, Washington. There, viewers can ogle the largest gathering of migrant shorebirds south of coastal Alaska. The northward flood tides of avian migrants in spring include other kinds of birds, such as pelicans, seabirds, swallows, and songbirds.

Spring is also wildflower season. After a rainy winter, the spectacle begins in northern Baja and southern California with hillsides abloom in California poppies, lupine, and other flowers. Vernal pools and ponds—essentially giant puddles left by the winter rains on impermeable clay soils—host a unique wild-flower show. As these ephemeral water sources dry out, annual plants germinate and flower in concentric circles around their edges, painting the cracked mud of shorelines with rings of vivid color. Farther north, Douglas' iris, with long, ruffled falls and clear purple color making it the prettiest of the coast's several species of wild iris, blooms from April to June in pockets of rich soil in coastal grasslands and meadows.

The fragrant and flammable chaparral that clothes the dry slopes from Baja California north to southern Oregon bursts into bloom in late winter and spring. Look first in the coastal sage scrub at low elevations along the coast in southern California and Baja California for the magenta, blue, and purple flowers of the various sages (related to cooking sage, but not to sagebrush) and the bright orange flowers of bush monkeyflower, a wild relative of snapdragons. Uphill, on steep south-facing slopes, the twenty or so species of California lilac bloom from late March to early June, tinting whole hillsides with their sprays of tiny, honey-scented flowers in shades from the deepest cyan to nearly white.

By May, the wildflower show peaks on the central and northern coast when the rhododendrons bloom, crowding openings in dark, wet coniferous forests with masses of their pink, perfumed flowers. The third weekend in May, Florence, Oregon, holds its annual Rhododendron Festival, when wild rhodys bloom in colorful profusion along Highway 101, between Florence and Coos Bay.

From south to north, spring moves up the coast in cloudlike flocks of birds and colorful, fragrant expanses of wildflowers.

EELGRASS

Zostera marina

Eelgrass (Zostera marina)

Nature is not a place to visit, it is home. . . .
—Gary Snyder, *The Practice of the Wild*

RANGE: The Pacific Coast, from Alaska south to Baja California; also the Atlantic Coast and Europe

HABITAT: Protected marine locations just below the low-tide line, including sandbanks, shallow channels, and silty or muddy bottoms in estuaries

NAME: Eelgrass is named for its slender, grasslike leaf blades, but the plant is neither eel, nor grass. *Zostera*, "belt" or "band" in Greek, refers to the straplike leaves; *marina*, "of the sea" in Latin, to the plant's saltwater habitat.

SIZE: The leaves grow as long as four feet but are only one-eighth to one-fourth of an inch wide, rising from a rhizome or underground stem up to nine feet long

COLOR: Bright green, but may be tinted red or brown by the coating of microscopic lives that inhabit the leaf blades

IMAGINE A CACOPHONY OF GABBLING VOICES so loud you must shout to be heard over the din. This is the scene at Padilla Bay, in Washington's Puget Sound, in winter and early spring, when thousands of black brant geese descend on the muddy tide flats and fertile shallows with the whistling of uncountable beating wings. The shallow bay looks like a bustling avian lunch counter. What lures the hordes of grazing geese? Under the water's surface grows a verdant meadow, acres upon acres of emerald-green leaf blades swaying gently with the movement of the sea. This subtidal meadow is a nursery for aquatic lives, home to billions of creatures, from microscopic diatoms to harbor seals. More fecund than the most productive terrestrial agricultural land, it literally gives life to the surrounding ocean, and thus to humans as well.

The "grass" that forms the meadow and supports its prodigious abundance is eelgrass, a flowering plant that, despite its name, is not a grass at all, but rather a close relative to freshwater pond weeds. Eelgrass is an oddity, a descendant of seed-producing land plants that recolonized saltwater environments. (Plant evolution in general is thought to have moved the other way, from sea to land: algae, the largest and most diverse group of marine plants, are considered the ancestors of terrestrial plants.)

The life of an eelgrass meadow such as Padilla Bay is seasonal. In winter, the plants are quiescent, their stems buried in the muck beneath the bay. In spring, as the days grow longer and the ocean water warms, the dormant meadow is reborn. Buried rhizomes sprout green leaf blades growing toward the light at the water's surface. The flat surfaces of the emerald blades are soon colonized by swarms of microscopic and near-microscopic lives, like epiphytes growing on jungle trees: diatoms, algae, feathery hydroid colonies, and moss animals or bryozoans—colonial marine animals that form crustlike, bushy, or coral-like growths. These minute creatures color the eelgrass blades with their crowded bodies. Algae tint the blades red; diatoms impart an olive-brown furry coating. Soon, protozoans, microscopic worms, and small crustaceans arrive to feed on earlier colonizers.

These, in turn, attract other grazers and browsers, and hunters. Tiny bubble snails creep over the encrusted leaves, scraping away algae with their radula, a tonguelike appendage studded with filelike "teeth." Minute mussels settle on the blades, as do amphipods, tiny shrimplike crustaceans, snagging food that drifts by. Jellyfish smaller than thimbles affix themselves upside down to the leaf surfaces, their short, stinging tentacles aimed upward. Miniature sea anemones settle on the eelgrass blades as well. Two-inch-long endemic sea slugs graze the leaves, their emerald color and longitudinal streaks mimicking the plant's pigment and its parallel leaf veins. Pipefish, long, slender relatives of sea horses, swim between the leaves on the hunt for small crustaceans and larval fish; they look just like swaying, drifting sections of iridescent green blades but for their big eyes—and their quick mouth.

By summer, the eelgrass blades have reached their four-foot maximum length, the plants have bloomed and released their seeds to drift on the currents, and life in the underwater meadow is in full swing. Clams dig into the sediments around the tightly packed rhizomes, filtering food from the water; brittle stars and starfish creep between the blades, ingesting small prey. Crabs—including succulent Dungeness crab—scuttle over and under the leaves. Surfperches, fingerling salmon, young herring, and other fish small enough to maneuver among the closely spaced plants feast on the epiphytes attached to the eelgrass leaves. Gulls walk through the beds at low tide, searching for crabs. Terns fly above the meadows, diving into the swaying blades to snatch fish. Sea otters swim through, hunting for crabs and clams. Harbor seals feed in the fecund meadows; gray whales swim in to eat shrimp. Bears and foxes hunt the beds at low tide.

As the days grow shorter again in autumn, eelgrass leaves die back and slowly decompose, enriching the water and sea bottom with their nutrients. The populations of tiny lives peak as they feed on the detritus and on each other. Now come hordes of migrating birds: sandpipers and other shorebirds, ducks, and geese. They sweep in by the thousands and hundreds of thousands, feasting noisily and intensely. Some remain only a few days and then head farther south; others, like the black brant at Padilla Bay, stay until early spring. Peregrine falcons dive into the avian flocks for meals, scattering birds everywhere.

The largest and most productive eelgrass beds are in estuaries, the tidal marshes where freshwater rivers and streams meet the ocean. These are among the most fertile ecosystems on earth, and also the least appreciated, perhaps because their phenomenal abundance lies hidden beneath the water's surface. Scientists estimate that the mean annual production of a marine estuary is eight times as great as that of a good cornfield, yet some 215 million acres of the world's estuaries—an area larger than the state of Texas—have been diked and filled, polluted with industrial wastes and agricultural runoff, and used as dumps. These ecosystems are the breadbaskets of our coasts, nurturing and sheltering the young of many marine lives—including fish, clams, oysters, crabs, shrimps, and lobsters. In their natural state, estuaries function better than any man-made flood control or pollution control design, slowing down the water flowing through them, absorbing flood crests, and trapping pollutants in their bottom muds.

We often think of nature as a frill, something like a beautiful landscape or a curious animal that we may admire or find interesting, but that has no bearing on our everyday lives. The lesson of Padilla Bay and other estuarine marshes is that we are woven into the web along with all of the other lives, from diatoms and eelgrass to salmon and black brant geese. Break the strands and eventually our lives will go too. We forget, at our peril, that nature is the air we breathe, the water we drink, the food we eat—it truly is our home.

Rough-skinned Newt

Taricha granulosa

There are hundreds of them moving at any one time, thousands of them, although they are hard to see; their skinny little backs are the color of oak leaves that have spent the winter at the bottom of a creek. . . . Moving through the forests, always toward the water, sometimes walking two, three kilometers, the female newts finally tumble over the bank of the creek or push through marsh grass and fall into the pond.

—Kathleen Dean Moore,
Riverwalking: Reflections on Moving Water

RANGE: From Santa Cruz, California, north to southeastern Alaska, mostly in Coast Ranges, from sea level to nine thousand feet in elevation

HABITAT: Moist forests and grasslands; breeds in ponds, lakes, and slow-moving streams

NAME: *Newt,* a corruption of "an ewt," comes from *eft* or *ewt,* the Old English words for these salamanders; these are "rough-skinned" newts for the granular bumps that make their back skin feel like sandpaper. The meaning of *Taricha* is obscure; *granulosa,* "grainy," in Latin, again refers to their skin texture.

SIZE: Adults to nearly seven inches long, of which half is tail

COLOR: Olive-green, brown, or blackish above, yellow to orange below; eyes silvery

NOTES: Rough-skinned newts are North America's most poisonous amphibian.

ON WARM, SOGGY SPRING DAYS, when tree trunks turn black with stem flow, branches bend under their burden of water, and mosses ooze like wet sponges, rough-skinned newts emerge to heed the call of the rain. These curious amphibians leave their terrestrial homes—rock piles, the undersides of logs, rotten wood, and the burrows of pocket gophers and other rodents—and march determinedly for the water in which they were born to breed.

Impelled by hormonal changes within their small, stubby bodies, hundreds of thousands of newts set out walking, steadily, undeterred by obstacles, whether downed tree trunks, fences, or highways and roads, guided to their destination by the earth's magnetic fields and their mental map of the landscape. (In some areas where newt migration routes cross roads, "Newt Xing" signs are posted and temporary road closures enforced to prevent mass annihilation under car tires.) Their pilgrimage is so urgent, writes Kathleen Dean Moore in *Riverwalking*, "If you pick one up, she will ... keep moving her legs in the same steady rhythm, plodding onward into the air."

Males get the itch first, setting out for their natal pond, marsh, or stream as early as December. (In southern California, the similar California newt of the Coastal Ranges lights out as soon as rains moisten that parched landscape.) Like the hero of any journey, a male rough-skinned newt is transformed by his pilgrimage: the grainy skin of his back becomes smooth and slimy, his tail flattens vertically for swimming, his cloaca—the combined opening for bodily wastes and sexual activity—swells, sperm mature in his testes, the skin under his arms and toes grows hard and callused, and his belly skin turns positively fluorescent orange. When a male reaches the home of his birth, he slides into the water and hangs there, facing the shore, head and legs dangling, for days or even weeks, suspended, seemingly inert. His brain waves are so flat that by human standards he would be dead.

Female rough-skinned newts set out on the same journey, but a few months later than males. Up and down over the forest floor they plod, aiming for their natal waters. When a female arrives at her destination and slips into the water, her presence hits the male like an electrical shock, charging his brain with a storm of activity. Impelled by desire, he swims swiftly over to her. He bumps into her, then clambers atop her, pulling her close under him with all four legs. She writhes and twists like an underwater bronc, but the rough skin of his toes and his underlegs gives him a tenacious grip. Now and then he thumps on her stomach with his hind legs, and she struggles more. One such pair may draw the attention of other males, which one by one clamber atop the male of the pair and attempt to dislodge him. Sometimes they accumulate, male atop male atop male, until, twisting in a writhing embrace with the female in its center, as many as fifty newts form a spinning wheel in the water.

If the latecomers cannot dislodge the first suitor, they eventually drift off, searching for other available females. Alone, the pair drift in their embrace for hours, occasionally rising to the surface to gulp a breath of air, the male periodically thumping the female and rubbing his chin on her head. Finally, a day or more later, they sink to the bottom, where the male walks in front of his mate and exudes a packet of sperm. The female sucks it up in her cloaca and they go their separate ways—or he may climb atop her and begin the dance again.

Afterward, the female rough-skinned newt wanders the muddy pond or stream bottom. Whenever she bumps into an aquatic plant, she grasps the stem with all four legs—much as the male grasped her—and lays one or two round, glassy eggs until she has spent her cache.

The eggs hatch in a few weeks, releasing tiny, tadpolelike larvae that swim the waters consuming anything that moves: insect larvae, baby fish, smaller amphibian larvae, and even each other. At the end of their first summer, surviving larvae sprout legs and emerge from their pond or stream to head into the forest after their parents. Those that persevere through the winter on land head back to the water to breed the following spring.

Rough-skinned newts are the most conspicuous salamanders of the moist forests along the Pacific Coast, especially in spring. With hundreds of them padding across the forest floor in plain view and thousands floating, nearly comatose, near the surface of a pond, it seems like they'd be scarfed up by hungry foxes, weasels, great blue herons, largemouth bass, garter snakes, or other flesheaters. But the little amphibians go on their way, largely unmolested, because they carry a deadly poison in the granular skin bumps that give them their name. When an animal ingests some of this toxic substance, its nervous system quits sending messages and its body shuts down—for good. Oregon's Coquille Indians are said to have used newt meat in preparing stew for their enemies. In his book *Wintergreen,* Robert Michael Pyle tells the story of the logger who was dared to drink a newt in his beer. He did, and died three hours later.

Like monarch butterflies, sea anemones, blister beetles, and other creatures that protect themselves with toxic substances, rough-skinned newts advertise their toxicity with bright coloration. Threatened, a newt arches its back until its tail touches its head and turns up its legs, rolling its body backward into a bright orange or yellow ball of flesh that shouts: "I'm toxic! Don't eat me!"

When the warm rains of spring summon newts from their damp terrestrial refuges, these small, stout amphibians set out on their treks, headed for the place where their lives began. It is one of the most reliable rituals of spring in the moist Coast Range forests: the rains come, the newts walk, life continues.

CALIFORNIA POPPY

Copa de oro
Eschscholzia californica

California POPPY
(Eschscholzia
californica)

When gold seekers flocked to California in 1849, they did not take long to find their own golden mementos of this new land. They pressed the California poppy and sent the dried flowers in their letters home.

—Karen B. Nilsson, *A Wildflower by Any Other Name*

Range: Native west of the Sierra Nevada and Cascade ranges, from southern California to southern Washington

Habitat: Dry grasslands and coastal hills up to two thousand feet in elevation

Name: The California poppy is named for the state in which it was first described; it is a member of the poppy family. *Copa de oro,* the name given it by Spanish Californians, means "cup of gold." *Eschscholzia* commemorates the friendship between poet and naturalist Adelbert von Chamisso, who collected and described the plant, and surgeon Johann Friedrich Gustave von Eschscholt.

Size: Flowers one to two inches across with four fan-shaped petals; plant eight to twenty-four inches high

Color: Foliage bluish-green and finely dissected; flower petals variable—deep orange, gold, and yellow, or sometimes cream with orange at the base

Notes: California poppies are the state flower of California.

California poppies are legendary in California for their masses of blossoms, which appear as if from nowhere to color miles and miles of the coastal and Central Valley landscapes. "Once upon a time," writes Charles Francis Saunders in his 1933 book, *Western Wildflowers and Their Stories,* "the attention of the traveler by sea along the southern California coast in late winter or early spring would be attracted by a remarkable spectacle. For mile upon mile the dimpled foothills of the Coast Range and its seaward stretching mesas would glow as if on fire from the limitless fields of copper-hued poppies; open mouthed to the sun."

Sadly, this extravagant spectacle is rare along the coast nowadays, although California poppies and other wildflowers still paint the hillsides of the Central Valley with their intense hues in late winter and early spring after sufficient winter rains. Where they appear, these colorful wildflower carpets are vivid reminders of the fields of gold that so captured Californian's hearts that the legislature named the California poppy the state flower in 1903. But the fiery poppy displays of the southern coast are a thing of the past, displaced by development and exotic landscaping.

Those coastal fields of gold were part of a plant community beautifully adapted to the central irony of the climate of the southern Pacific Coast: despite an abundance of water *off*shore, almost no rain falls *on*shore for six months of the year, during what would be the main growing season. In winter, the generally southeasterly flow of polar air brings storm after storm to the Pacific Coast, leaving the land awash in water (sometimes literally, as whole hillsides let loose and slide into the ocean). But beginning in spring, the prime growing season, an area of high pressure over the Pacific Ocean moves north and deflects the moisture-bearing polar airflow from reaching the southern coast. For long months, cold ocean currents generate fog banks along the shore, but no rain.

Where the fog is dense and persistent near the ocean, plants such as coast redwoods thrive in its blanket of moisture; farther from the coast, where fog is less dependable and sun and wind combine to dry out the soil more quickly, California poppies and other members of their coastal prairie community must survive long months of drought. These plants thus have adopted the strategy of desert plants: after winter rains, they sprout their blue-gray foliage quickly and bloom extravagantly, living with abandon while the moisture in the soil lasts, then dying back as soon as drought sets in. Unlike the desert's annual wildflowers, however, California poppies are perennials, sprouting year after year from the same roots. Although the poppy blossoms appear as if by magic, the plants have been there all along, hidden underground.

Spanish Californians called California poppies *dormideras*, or "sleepy ones," since the flowers open in the morning and close when the sun sets or on cloudy days. The blossoms' sun-loving habits echo those of their pollinators, beetles active only on warm, sunny days. The flowers save energy by closing when conditions aren't conducive for their partners in reproduction. California poppy flowers are designed with beetles in mind: they emit a spicy fragrance that attracts the pollen-feeding insects; they open wide and grow close together, making access to and movement from flower to flower easy for the somewhat clumsy pollen-dusted beetles; and they grow in masses, providing a protein-rich food resource irresistible to their partners.

Like their cousins, the opium poppies, California poppies' watery sap contains narcotic substances. Unlike opium, however, California poppies' narcotics are relatively mild. These plants were used in traditional medicine, reports Charles Francis Saunders. California Indians used the root to soothe toothaches; a liniment of the plant's sap was also used to treat headaches; the Luiseño Indians of the San Diego area made a chewing gum that included the flowers. The first European explorer to collect this eye-catching plant was Archibald Menzies, surgeon and naturalist of Captain George Vancouver's expedition to the Pacific Coast from 1791 to 1795. Menzies gave California poppy seeds to the Royal Botanical Garden at Kew, England. Unfortunately, the plants that sprouted in England's damp and cloudy climate failed to blossom and thus could not be described for science.

Imagine bringing California's state flower and its coastal prairie community back to the hills of the southern and central coast by planting backyards and public landscapes alike with these beautiful and tough natives instead of with exotic species. Then imagine whole hillsides glowing as if on fire from countless California poppy blossoms, returning their native magic to the California coast.

BLACK OYSTERCATCHER

Haematopus bachmani

Black Oystercatcher
(Haematopus bachmani)

Where the Pacific Ocean breaks against rocky shorelines, pairs of these big black birds stalk about on the rocks and nearby flats. If disturbed, they take flight with loud, ringing whistles easily heard above the sound of the waves.

—Kenn Kaufman, *Lives of North American Birds*

RANGE: Year-round resident of the Pacific Coast, from the
Aleutian Islands south to Baja California, Mexico

HABITAT: Rocky coasts and undisturbed sea islands

NAME: Black oystercatchers are named for their all-black
plumage and their diet of bivalves. *Haematopus*, "blood
foot" in Greek, refers to their bright pinkish feet and legs;
bachmani honors the Reverend Charles Bachman of
Columbia, South Carolina, a friend of John James
Audubon, who described the bird in 1838.

SIZE: Adult birds sixteen and one-half to eighteen and one-half
inches long, beak to tail tip, and weighing about one and
one-half pounds

COLOR: Adults jet-black with startlingly orange beak and pink
legs and feet, juveniles brown with a dusky beak, eggs buff
and spotted with dark brown

VOICE: A loud, piping "wink! wink!" alarm call, or a soft "pee-
ah" whistle when flying

ON SPRING VACATIONS OF MY CHILDHOOD, my grandfather
sometimes took my mother, my brother, and me to a rocky beach
north of San Francisco to go tide-pooling. The memories of those
long-ago expeditions come rushing back whenever I smell seaweed drying on tidal rocks, feel the shock of the cold surf, or hear
the loud, piping voices of black oystercatchers.

Black oystercatchers are as characteristic of rocky shores
along the Pacific Coast as tide pools. So strong is these shorebirds'
association, in fact, that they are only missing from the sandy
beaches and shale bluffs of southern California.

On rocky shores, dense colonies of mussels and barnacles

band the rocks just below the high-tide line. This rich food resource is a black oystercatcher's niche, but a difficult one to exploit: the rocks are slippery with algae and wave spray, they provide no shelter from aerial or waterborne predators, and the oncoming tides can catch one unawares. These big shorebirds are well-adapted to their habitat, however. Strong legs with long-toed feet give them good purchase on the wave-washed rocks, and a heavy body insulates them against the constant chill. But most important, they possess a bill perfectly adapted to opening shellfish. More than twice as long as a black oystercatcher's head, and sharp-edged, each mandible of the bird's beak is triangular in cross section and tapers from head to tip. The result is a slender but extremely rigid and strong tool, as useful as the best oysterman's knife. With their specialized bill, these birds can open a shellfish in less than thirty seconds. Remember that the next time you struggle with an oyster!

These shorebirds are either stabbers or hammerers. Stabbers are stealthy: they sneak up on open mussels or other mollusks and plunge their beak between the two shells, severing the powerful adductor muscles that would otherwise snap the halves of the shell tightly closed. Once the muscles are disabled, the mollusk is defenseless. The oystercatcher then simply chisels out the succulent meat and eats it. Hammerers use brute force: they first loosen the whole shell from the rock, then, with a series of sharp blows, they break a hole in one shell. They reach through the hole and cut the adductor muscles, open the shell, and pluck out the meat. Young oystercatchers learn one or the other technique— but not both—from their parents.

Whether stabbers or hammerers, these birds feed at low tide, and loaf or sleep on the onshore part of their territory at high tide. When mussels or clams are in short supply, they turn to limpets and barnacles. (Despite their name, black oystercatchers forage on rocky shores, not on the sandy bottoms where oysters grow. Thus, they rarely eat oysters.) They also consume crabs, sea urchins, and beetle larvae. In winter, black oystercatchers often move to tidal mudflats. There they probe the soft soil for marine worms and other invertebrates. Like other shorebirds, they may be able to feel the vibrations of buried prey with the sensitive tip of their bill.

From spring through fall, pairs of black oystercatchers maintain a feeding and breeding territory: a ledge well above the high-tide line and adjacent subtidal shellfish beds. These long-lived birds—banded oystercatchers have survived as long as sixteen years—mate for life. Each spring, the pair returns to their territory and loudly declares their fiefdom: the two birds stand together on a prominent point, call in their loud, piping whistle, then rotate 180 degrees and call again. Or they run along side by side, all the time broadcasting their carrying call. The pair may also take off and circle their breeding territory, piping the limits of their domain.

After mating, the male builds their nest, a simple scraped-out bowl on the ground, filled with tiny rock and shell flakes. The female lays one to three eggs in the bowl; the eggs hatch about four weeks later. Like most ground-nesting birds, black oyster-catcher young are precocial—that is, mobile within hours of birth. The young develop quickly: they run and swim by the time they are three days old, begin foraging for food at ten days, and fly at just a little over a month. But they stay with their parents until the following breeding season, perfecting their skills as stabbers or hammerers. (Most juvenile birds are independent within a month or so of fledging. Perhaps because of the length of time needed to learn their shellfish harvesting technique, the black oystercatcher's adolescence is much longer.)

The Aleut Indian names for black oystercatchers, "he-gich!" or "heck!", sound just like their carrying call. Hearing the piping voices of a pair of black oystercatchers brings me back to spring vacations of my childhood, along with the smell of seaweed and the feel of the surf.

GIANT PACIFIC OCTOPUS

Octopus dofleini

Giant Pacific
OCTOPUS
(Octopus dofleini)

Then the creeping murderer, the octopus, steals out, slowly, softly, moving like a gray mist, pretending now to be a bit of weed, now a rock, now a lump of decaying meat while its evil goat eyes watch coldly. It oozes and flows toward a feeding crab. . . . [S]uddenly it runs lightly on the tips of its arms, as ferociously as a charging cat. It leaps savagely on the crab, there is a puff of black fluid, and the struggling mass is obscured in the sepia cloud while the octopus murders the crab.

—John Steinbeck, *Cannery Row*

RANGE: Alaska to southern California
HABITAT: Rocky areas, from tide pools at the low-tide line to as deep as 1,650 feet on the ocean bottom
NAME: Giant Pacific octopuses are the largest octopus on the Pacific Coast, and among the largest of their kind. *Octopus,* Greek for "eight-footed," refers to the eight legs that distinguish these cephalopods; *dofleini* most likely commemorates the discoverer of this enormous octopus species.
SIZE: As long as twenty feet from head to end of leg; the record specimen weighed nearly six hundred pounds
COLOR: Reddish or brownish, but can change to bright red, black, or near white
NOTES: Giant Pacific octopuses are fished commercially from Alaska to northern California.

OCTOPUSES, ALONG WITH MANTA RAYS AND SHARKS, get a bad rap. In *Twenty Thousand Leagues Under the Sea,* for instance, Jules Verne has enormous octopuses attack the *Nautilus,* Captain Nemo's submarine. The largest of these "devilfish" bites off the propeller to stop the ship. (Although Verne calls his imaginary beasts "squid," what he describes are octopuses with eight arms and rounded heads.) In *Cannery Row,* Steinbeck's octopus is a "murderer," its evil goat eyes watching "coldly" for prey. What is it about octopuses that causes us to withdraw, our flesh crawling, when we see a sucker-studded tentacle emerge from beneath a rock?

Perhaps it is their nocturnal habits. Octopuses are creatures of the twilight and darkness, spending the daylight hours in their dens in cracks in underwater rocks, holes, sunken ships, or other hiding places. Or perhaps it is their grotesque appearance, their bulbous head with its protuberant eyes, their wrinkled, flaccid skin, their eight long arms with twin rows of fleshy suction cups below. Whatever causes our revulsion, when we shrink away we miss the real creature, a graceful animal with considerable intelligence, communicating through body language and swift changes of color.

The octopus, wrote Edward Ricketts (the real-life model for "Doc" in *Cannery Row*) in his book *Between Pacific Tides,* "has eyes as highly developed as ours, and a larger and better-functioning brain than any other invertebrate animal." These cephalopods use that brain to hunt shrimps, crabs, scallops, abalones, clams, various fish, and smaller octopods. Bivalves and crabs are favorite foods.

A giant Pacific octopus on the hunt glides along the ocean floor with a catlike motion, exploring the bottom with its sensitive tentacles, each covered with two rows of suckers, around 240 per arm. The tentacles feel textures like eight enormous fingers, and taste flavors like multiple tongues. Octopuses depend on their acute vision, much like humans do, to determine sizes, shapes, and distances between objects. Unlike humans, octopuses can raise their eyes out of their heads like periscopes; they look at the undersea world through rectangular pupils.

When a giant Pacific octopus detects its prey, it darts over, gliding smoothly on all eight legs, grabs the prey with its two foremost tentacles, and draws up the center of its suckers to create a nearly unbreakable grip (it takes forty pounds of pressure to release the grip of a three-pound octopus). It bites the prey with the beaked mouth under its mantle, the skirtlike skin below its head, and injects a paralyzing poison. (If the prey is in a shell, the octopus first rasps a hole in the shell with its toothed radula, or tongue.) A giant Pacific octopus then carries the limp prey back to its den to eat, and piles the empty shells just outside the den entrance.

Grotesque at rest, a giant Pacific octopus on the hunt is eerily graceful. "Never did the . . . octopuses seem so beautiful and so worthy of consideration as when we watched them 'walking' on the bottom," wrote Jacques-Yves Cousteau and Philippe Diolé in *Octopus and Squid: The Soft Intelligence*. Their fluid gait "is neither a crawl or a slide, but an extremely supple motion whose component parts are difficult to determine. The animal goes forward, its arms stretched in the shape of a fan, as though he were exploring what lay ahead. The first two dorsal arms are extended; the next two follow . . . while the body is carried at a slant."

Tentacles, suckers, and gliding motion aside, what is most unusual about an octopus is its color. When at rest, a giant Pacific octopus blends into its background in hues of muddy brown. But when it sights prey, the octopus may turn bright red, as if gripped by strong emotion. When threatened, it may go pale white, or turn black. Or the octopus may flash spots or stripes like a neon sign. These lightning-swift color changes—an octopus can go from white to red in less than a second—are part of octopuses' language. Although color-blind themselves, octopuses "speak" with color, which they see as brightness. (They do not make sounds.) Chromatophores, elastic bags holding red, yellow, orange, blue, or black pigments, cover octopuses' skin. To change color, the octopus contracts the muscles around the bags, making them appear as large spots; when the muscles relax, the spots fade. To turn red, for instance, an octopus tightens the muscles around its orange and red chromatophores.

Despite their size and formidable tentacles, giant Pacific octopuses are vulnerable to predators, including humans, seals, sea otters, sharks, and other large fish. An octopus' first response to danger is to flee and hide, deforming its rubbery body—even its head changes shape, and its eyes can move obliquely—to squeeze into what seem like impossibly small spaces. In fact, an eight-foot-long octopus can fit through an opening the diameter of a one-pound coffee can. When flight is impossible, octopuses bluff their attacker, bristling their skin, flashing colors, and raising their tentacles in a threat posture. If that fails, an octopus shoots out a cloud of dense, dark fluid from an "ink sac" near its anus. When the confused predator grasps at the phantom octopus, the real one glides away.

Courtship between any two individuals in a species where larger members eat smaller ones is a decidedly touchy affair. Male octopuses signal their intentions by flashing colors or stripes, or raising their tentacles in threatlike postures, as if to say "I'm too big to be lunch, but I'd make a good mate!" Mating itself is conducted at arm's length, as it were: A male with mating on his mind reaches under his mantle and fills his copulatory organ, an enlarged tentacle that develops at breeding age, with a packet of spermatozoa. He then bluffs his intended into docility, reaches under her mantle, deposits the packet, and glides away.

His mate has a long ordeal ahead. Within days, she lays clusters of rice-grain-sized eggs, about eighty thousand in all, on the roof of her den. She tends the eggs—often not eating or leaving the den—for five or six months as the embryos within develop into tiny octopuses. Once the babies, minute versions of their parents, struggle out of the egg sacs and swim off, they are on their own. (Their emaciated mother usually dies soon after.) Few baby giant Pacific octopuses survive to adulthood, but those that do grow into graceful creatures with arms as long as twenty feet, gliding through the dim ocean depths.

CALIFORNIA GRUNION

Leuresthes tenuis

California Grunion
(Leuresthes tennis)

When Buster [the hermit crab] is running around for all he's worth, I can only presume it's high tide in Tucson. With or without evidence, I'm romantic enough to believe it. This is the lesson of Buster, the poetry that camps outside the halls of science: Jump for joy, hallelujah. Even a desert has tides.

—Barbara Kingsolver, *High Tide in Tucson*

RANGE: From San Francisco, California, to Baja California, Mexico; most commonly seen south of Morro Bay

HABITAT: Sandy beaches and offshore waters to a depth of about sixty feet

NAME: California grunion hail from that state; *grunion* comes from the Spanish word *gruñon*, or "grunter," perhaps a reference to the effort required to dig their spawning holes on beaches. *Leuresthes*, "smooth garment" in Greek, refers to the fish's smooth scales; *tenuis*, Greek for "thin" or "slender," to its slight build.

SIZE: Up to seven and one-half inches long, about the size of a smelt

COLOR: Greenish above and silvery below, with a pale stripe lining their sides

IN *HIGH TIDE IN TUCSON*, Barbara Kingsolver tells the story of Buster, the hermit crab she unknowingly brought home in a conch shell from the Bahamas. Ensconced in a terrarium, Buster developed regular—but inexplicable—cycles, alternating times of inactivity with episodes of manic energy. Kingsolver was at a loss to explain his behavior until she remembered research by F. A. Brown, "the grandfather of the biological clock."

In 1954, Brown took some oysters from Connecticut to his laboratory in Chicago to study their biological cycles. For the first two weeks, the oysters behaved according to their usual tidal cycles from the faraway Connecticut shore. Then their behavior—still in unison, still as regular as the tides—shifted. The researchers were mystified, until, writes Kingsolver, "It dawned on [them] after some calculations that the oysters were responding to high tide in Chicago. Never mind that the gentle mollusks lived in glass boxes in the basement of a steel-and-cement building. Nor that Chicago has no ocean." Buster the hermit crab was, like the transplanted oysters, responding to what would be tidal cycles in his new home: the Sonoran Desert.

It makes sense that creatures living in the tide wash, like crabs and oysters, would be governed by the regular in-out cycle: when the sea flows in, food is abundant, temperatures are clement, and, for those breathing through gills, oxygen is available. When the tide is out, the shore is essentially a salty desert, exposed to the desiccating effects of sun and wind, unprotected from the wide diurnal temperature swings, and lacking the floating soup of nutrients supplied by the ocean. But what astonishes me is how precise the calibrations are to the swing of the tides. Take the California grunion, one of a number of kinds of ocean fish that spawn on a tidal clock. In the dark of the night a few days after the full moon in March, April, May, and June—during the second-highest high tides of each monthly cycle—female grunion swim out of the ocean and up onto the beach to lay their eggs in the sand. The female rides the breaking waves right up out of the water into the alien environment of the air, then digs into the soupy sand with her tail. In a matter of about thirty seconds—before she runs out of air—she lays some two thousand eggs in the resultant three-inch-deep pit, while a male grunion arches around her and sprays his milt over her cache. Then both slip back into the sea with the next wave.

The eggs, buried under more sand by subsequent tides, remain above the reach of the waves until the new moon brings the spring tides—the highest high tides of each month—ten days to two weeks later. This extra-high water washes out the eggs, which hatch on immersion, releasing tiny grunion larvae by the millions to swim out to sea under cover of darkness. The young fish eat and grow for a year, spawning the spring after they hatch. A female grunion may spawn four to eight times in a season; few survive to spawn the next year. Grunion, like other small fish, are the lunch meat of the oceans, the basic food for a wide variety of predators, including gulls, terns, pelicans, larger fish, seals and other pinnipeds, and humans.

The most astonishing thing about grunion spawning is the fine timing of their run up the beach. Some impulse tells them to spawn after the full moon, not during the very highest high tides of the month. This way none but the highest high tides can reach their eggs, and those come at just the right interval—ten to fourteen days—to hatch the young and wash them out to sea. How do California grunion judge the time and the tides? Perhaps the same mechanism that synchronizes women's menstrual cycles to the phases of the moon. We do not know enough to explain the phenomena.

When hordes of California grunion swim up onto the beaches on their spawning nights, they attracts hordes of humans. People line the sand, scooping the silvery fish up with their hands, their hats, buckets, or whatever will hold them (a fishing license is required), then cook their catch over beach fires. I prefer to just watch the show, amazed by the tidal clock these fish possess, a precisely tuned mechanism that urges them to swim ashore on only the correct nights, impelled out of their home environment just long enough to lay the seeds of the next generation. As I watch a female grunion thrash in the wet sand, my body reminds me that the grunion and I—and Buster the crab—are all related, tuned to the cycles of the moon.

Red Abalone

Haliotis rufescens

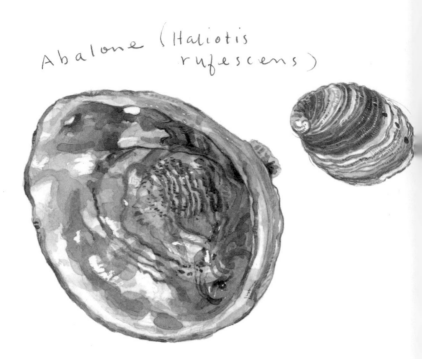

Abalone (Haliotis rufescens)

The very word "abalone" conjures up a host of associations for the Californian who has accustomed himself to steaks from this delicious shellfish. Still more vivid memories of foggy dawns will be recalled by the sportsman who has captured this huge, limpetlike snail on the low-tide rocks and reefs. Alas, they are no longer common intertidally. . . .

—Edward F. Ricketts, et al., *Between Pacific Tides*

RANGE: From Central Oregon to central Baja California, Mexico; most common from Monterey Bay to San Luis Obispo, California

HABITAT: Rocks and rocklike substrates (concrete blocks, cars, sunken ships) on the ocean bottom as deep as 540 feet

NAME: Red abalone are named for the color of these mollusk's shells; *abalone* comes (through Spanish) from their Shoshone name, *aulun. Haliotis* means "sea dweller" in Greek; *rufescens* is Greek for "reddish."

SIZE: Adults' shells up to twelve inches across and broadly oval

COLOR: Outside of shell usually reddish, inside pearly iridescent in pinks, pale blues, and greens

NOTES: Red abalones are the largest North American abalones and thus the most prized commercially.

A RED ABALONE SHELL DECORATED the living room of my child-hood home, one of my mother's keepsakes from growing up near the San Francisco Bay. Its bumpy exterior and iridescent interior, pierced with a line of five perfectly round holes, fascinated me. I remember lying on the couch when I was sick—feverish and bored—and asking for the abalone shell. I held it to my ear to hear the ocean's roar, tilted it back and forth to watch the interior colors shift from silver to pink to green, and traced the cool, pearly surface with my fingers.

Abalones are mollusks, first cousins to snails. If you look closely at their shells, you can see the spiral form—like a flattened cinnamon roll—and the banding that denotes each season's growth. The animal inside looks more like an oversized limpet, with a powerful muscular "foot" that, along with the mucus the abalone secretes, allows it to cling tightly to its underwater substrate. The line of holes leading outward from near the center of the shell allows the animal to excrete wastewater when the shell itself is locked down to the rock like a calcareous fortress.

With their heavy shells and powerful suction, abalones pose a challenge to predators attracted by their size and succulent meat. Still, crabs, fish, sea stars, octopuses, sea otters, and humans manage to dislodge them. Cabezon, fish that live in kelp beds, bump small abalone hard with their head to dislodge them, then swallow the mollusk whole, regurgitating the shell after digesting the flesh. Sea otters use their teeth and strong forelimbs to pry up these shellfish; human divers use prybars. Their tight grip notwithstanding, abalones are by no means immobile. In fact, an abalone may escape a predator like a sunflower star or an octopus by "galloping" away, twisting its shell wildly from side to side, and secreting a screen of mucus to hide its retreat.

Like some snails, abalones are grazers, moving about on their underwater reefs, chewing algae fronds in situ or snagging broken-off pieces that drift by. (Abalone and most other mollusks possess a radula, a toothed, filelike tongue that allows them to scrape and chew. A chewing abalone makes a surprisingly loud crunching sound.) Abalone are messy enough eaters that a species of small, large-clawed shrimp, *Betaeus harfordi,* makes its living foraging for scraps among the folds in a mollusk's body. The shrimp rarely leaves its host, and apparently locates the abalone by smell, sensing a chemical emanating from its flesh.

The bands of a red abalone's shell reveals the occupant's diet. If the shell is striped with red or reddish-brown, the abalone has been consuming plenty of its preferred food, seaweed in the red alga family. The algae's pigments color the mollusk's shell. An abalone forced to subsist on seaweeds from the green or brown alga families will have a green or whitish shell; a shell with bands in differing colors says that the abalone dined on different kinds of seaweed at the times the various bands were secreted.

Red abalone are slow-growing, long-lived shellfish. It takes a young abalone four to six years to grow to four inches across; large ones may be twenty or more years old. They mature sexually at about six years, and sometime between February and April, red abalone spawn, releasing hordes of white sperm or gray-green eggs (depending on the sex of the parent) into the water. Sperm and eggs make contact by chance. The resulting larval abalone, which looks more like a ciliated bit of zooplankton than like its molluscan parents, drifts with the currents until stimulated to settle down. Chemicals secreted by adult abalones, marking a good place to attach and live, may be the impetus it needs to put down its foot, so to speak.

Populations of all eight Pacific Coast abalone species have dropped dramatically in the past few decades, partly due to over-harvesting, but also, especially on the southern coast, due to pollution and warm water discharges from nuclear power plants. (Abalone harvesters also blame the successful reestablishment of the sea otter, an important abalone predator, although those claims have not been substantiated.) Abalone have vanished from areas where they were once abundant—worse yet, say marine biologists, whole years have gone by when no young abalones survived to settle down and grow.

As abalones have grown scarcer, the price fetched for their meat on the market has soared: biologists say a diver can haul in $30,000 worth of abalone in one day from a dense colony. Diners may shell out hundreds of dollars for an abalone dinner. If you've ever had properly prepared abalone, you know the lure of this heavenly shellfish, fork-tender and delicious. (Proper preparation, however, is essential. The heavy muscle fibers of the foot must be pounded into tenderness. To quote that culinary bible, *Joy of Cooking:* "[Abalone] meat is ready to cook when it looks like Dalí's limp watch.")

Biologists working to reestablish abalones in places such as the Channel Islands National Park have built protected "abalone condos"—wire cages with stacks of concrete blocks inside stocked with young abalones—on offshore rock shelves in the hopes of increasing the mollusk's reproductive success. So valuable are the residents of the cages that the locations of the colonies are kept secret.

Thinking of my mother's abalone shell, collected fifty years ago on the central California coast, when abalones were still abundant under rocks in wading distance from shore, the problem is clear: too many people, too much competition for space and resources. The same goes for California spiny lobsters, Dungeness crabs, salmon, least terns, snowy plovers, redwood trees, and many other Pacific Coast lives. As cartoonist Walt Kelly's Pogo said: "We have met the enemy and he is us." The question is, what will we do?

Ceanothus thyrsiflorus

Blueblossom
(Ceanothus thyrsiflorus)

As for me, when someone who isn't from Southern California complains about our dry, brushy hills, I want to take them out to that trail I mentioned earlier. I want to tell them to stand among the blooming ceanothus and the sage and take a deep breath. There it is, I'd say—the perfume of California.

—Peter Fish, "Chaparral," *Sunset* magazine

RANGE: Outer Coast Ranges, from southern Oregon to Santa
   Barbara County, California
HABITAT: Canyons and steep, dry slopes in chaparral, redwood,
   and mixed-evergreen forests to two thousand feet in elevation
NAME: *Blueblossom* is for the color of this shrub's flowers.
   Ceanothus, the name picked for the genus by Carl Linneaus,
   "the father of classification," is Greek for "thistle," an
   obscure reference; *thyrsiflorus,* "wand-flowered" in Greek,
   describes the shape of the flower clusters.
SIZE: Shrubs up to twenty feet tall, more commonly four to
   eight feet; evergreen leaves three-quarters to two inches
   long, oval with finely toothed margins; flowers clustered in
   sprays to three inches long
COLOR: Leaves waxy green; flowers light to deep blue; bark
   reddish-brown

WHEN YOU SEE PHOTOS of whole hillsides aflame in southern
California, you are seeing chaparral, the area's most characteristic
plant community. (So emblematic is chaparral of the area that
Hollywood itself is named for a common chaparral plant,
California holly.) Like the *maquis* of the Mediterranean Coast,
chaparral is comprised of a dense, tangled cover of evergreen
shrubs that are adapted to both long periods of drought and frequent fire. Hillsides of chaparral appear dusty and dead for half
the year—from late spring until the winter rains—but they are
simply dormant, waiting for water. The perennial shrubs survive
the drought through sophisticated adaptations, including chemical defenses, physiological modifications, and partnerships with

fungi and algae in the soil.

Chaparral plants such as blueblossom coat their outer tissues with a wide variety of waxes and volatile oils, thus producing the aromatic odors that characterize this plant community. These compounds are more than just perfumes, however. They function as sunscreens (plants sunburn too), as vapor barriers to prevent loss of water and dehydration, and as an odd-tasting repellant for hungry browsers. Chaparral plants also slow down their metabolisms during the hot and dry months of summer and fall to conserve water. Most are evergreens that compensate for keeping their leaves all year with a host of adaptations to reduce heat gain and water loss: serrated or spiny edges increase surface area, thus dissipating heat without absorbing significantly more sunlight; in-rolled leaves trap air and reduce evaporation; hairs on the leaf surface provide some shade, trap moving air, and also diffuse heat. Many chaparral shrubs also grow in association with mycorrhizae, the threadlike underground "roots" of fungus, that extend the plant's root system, allowing it to harvest additional nutrients and water from the soil. Other chaparral shrubs, including blueblossom, host microscopic nitrogen-fixing bacteria—which act like in-house fertilizer plants—in nodules in their roots.

In late spring, most chaparral shrubs burst into bloom, aiming to reproduce before the drought sets in. Blueblossom, the largest and one of the most widespread of some forty species of shrubs collectively called California lilac, transforms hillsides of dusty chaparral into fragrant flower gardens with its masses of blue, honey-scented blossoms. California lilacs got their name from their flower's resemblance to cultivated lilacs: all sprout clusters of tiny, perfumed blossoms in shades from white to purple.

Blueblossom and the various species of California lilac share other characteristics as well: all grow as twisting, multistemmed shrubs—some as ground-hugging mats, others taller than an adult human. All host nitrogen-fixing bacteria in their roots, making their tender new shoots very nutritious and important browse for many wild herbivores, especially deer. All sport small leaves—mostly evergreen—heavily coated with waxes to resist dehydration, and, most important to humans, all are highly flammable.

Fire and chaparral go together as surely as the wind and drought which render southern California's summers tinder-dry. The tissues of most chaparral shrubs are coated with combustible waxes and oils—some, like chamise, even give off explosive gases when they are heated. These shrubs also shed a "litter" of leaves, twigs, and bark, which accumulates and dries to incendiary kindling. But fire in the chaparral community has not always come in sweeping conflagrations that blacken everything in their path. Botanists who study the history of natural fire in chaparral believe that before the all-too-effective fire suppression of the past hundred years, chaparral burns were relatively small, ignited by lightning from summer storms. Their intensity was kept in check partly by fires deliberately set by the Native Americans and by the relatively high humidity in some areas in the summer months. Still, these fires might have burned for months, waxing and waning as natural fires do, sometimes flaring up, at other times smoldering and creeping along the soil surface. Because these historic fires were fairly frequent, occurring every fifteen years or so on any given site, fuels never built up to conflagration levels and recently burned patches served as firebreaks. Biologists believe that these fires created a mosaic of chaparral in different stages of succession—some patches young and nutritious with lots of edible fruits and seeds; others old and dense and tough; still others in between—providing diverse habitat for many kinds of wildlife.

After a century of fewer fires and more human settlement, however, the chaparral country has grown into tough, nearly impenetrable thickets of incendiary shrubs underlain by a thick layer of combustible plant litter. Today's fires are most often human-caused and occur in the tinder-dry conditions of autumn, pushed down the canyons by the Santa Ana winds. Hence the conflagrations that blaze across television screens and the front pages of newspapers. After these catastrophic fires come the winter rains, which pour off the newly denuded slopes in destructive floods, carrying tons of soil.

Even after today's catastrophic fires, however, blueblossom and the other tough chaparral shrubs sprout within weeks after the flames die down, either from unburned roots or from fire-cracked seeds. The new green shoots grow swiftly and vigorously, fertilized by nutrients released by the fire. In some cases, wildflowers long thought vanished reappear after such burns. Two years after the Hondo Canyon blaze, which swept through the Santa Monica Mountains north of Los Angeles in 1994, for instance, the slopes blazed gold with fire poppies, wildflowers that hadn't been seen in the area in fifty years.

"After a fire, people look up at these mountains and say destruction," says Rich Hawkins, fire and resource manager for the Angeles National Forest. "I look at them and think rejuvenation." That is the story of blueblossom and the chaparral where it grows: born in fire, growing, blooming, getting old, and eventually given new life by the flames.

PACIFIC MADRONE

Arbutus menziesii

Birds like to eat the berries in winter...

Pacific
MADRONE
(Arbutus menziesii)

Sitting on a little promontory, watching nighthawks circle in a sky the color of star sapphires, I felt as though my veins and nerves were grown into the ground, connected with tree roots. The faint red glimmer of a madrone trunk in the dusk of the rustle of last year's yellow leaves falling seemed as much as I needed out of life. . . . I was woven into the fabric of root and branch.

—David Rains Wallace, *The Klamath Knot*

RANGE: From near sea level to 4,500 feet in elevation in the
Coast Ranges, the Cascades, and the Sierra Nevada, from
British Columbia to southern California

HABITAT: Dry, rocky slopes below snow line in the north part of
its range to moist, mixed-evergreen forests in the south part
of its range

NAME: *Madrone* is from the Spanish *madroño*, the name for the
related strawberry tree of the Mediterranean. *Arbutus* is the
Latin name for the strawberry tree; *menziesii* commemorates Scottish botanist Archibald Menzies, who collected
specimens of this and many other Pacific Coast plant
species.

SIZE: Mature trees up to one hundred feet high, with a rounded
crown almost as wide as tall; leaves three to six inches long

COLOR: Bark reddish-brown and flaky, revealing yellow or
orange underbark; leaves leathery and bright green above,
dull gray-green below; flowers small, bell-shaped, and white
or pinkish

ON RAINY SPRING DAYS in Washington's Puget Sound country,
madrone trees stand out from the dark forest. The smooth upper
skin of their twisting trunks is a vivid hue of red-orange, one of
the few bright colors on gray days. Sometimes madrones grow
skinny and tall, their ropy, muscled limbs twisting like snakes to
reach through the forest canopy. Others' limbs sprout from one
side of the trunk like an umbrella turned inside out by the wind.
Still other madrones lie right on the ground, their huge trunks
creeping along for many feet before the massive branches stretch
upward.

The madrone's eccentric form isn't the only odd thing about
this unusual tree. Members of the Ericaceae, the heath family,

they are kin to rhododendrons, azaleas, huckleberries, manzanitas, heathers, and other familiar shrubs. They resemble their kin in most ways: madrones sport long, oval, shiny-topped evergreen leaves like rhododendrons; thin, peeling bark and clusters of bright red berries like manzanitas; and clusters of small, urn-shaped flowers like huckleberries and heathers. Yet, unlike these shrubs, madrones grow into sizable, spreading-crowned trees.

The Pacific madrone's dense, cherry-colored wood, weighing forty-four pounds per square foot, was once in demand by Spanish caballeros for stirrups, and by sailors for anchors. Today the hard, lustrous wood is rarely used commercially because it tends to warp and split as it dries. But these eccentric trees are used by wildlife: band-tailed pigeons and other birds eat the berries in winter; bees and other nectar-seeking insects search out the sweet flowers in summer.

Growing from British Columbia to the mountains of southern California, Pacific madrone pops up where you least expect it in a dizzying variety of habitats along almost the entire length of the coast. (It is the most northerly of evergreen hardwoods.) Where I knew it from the edges of Puget Sound, madrone was an indicator of dry conditions, rocky places, and well-drained soils. In Oregon's wide Willamette Valley, where soils dry out too much in summer to support conifers, madrone grows in grassy savannas with the lichen-draped forms of Oregon white oak. The open understory of these savannas was once maintained by frequent ground fires set by the area's Indian inhabitants to improve habitat for animals they hunted.

Farther south, madrone is part of the richly diverse tree community that forms the mixed-evergreen forests of the Coast Ranges and the Klamath Mountains, a remnant of the ancient temperate forests that flourished across the continent before frigid millennia of the Ice Ages. Unlike most of the coastal forests, dominated by one or two species, these forests are so diverse that their richness is overwhelming. In *The Klamath Knot,* David

Rains Wallace names the plants in a passage that becomes an incantation: "Douglas firs, grand firs, ponderosa and sugar pines, Port Orford cedars, and western hemlocks tower above; tan oaks, madrones, Garry, black, and goldencup oaks, golden chinquapins, bay laurels, and bigleaf maples form a broadleaf subcanopy; smaller trees such as Pacific dogwood, western yew, elderberry, cascara, buckeye, and hawthorn grow under that; a shrub layer of hazel, poison oak, wild rose, vine and Rocky Mountain maple, ceanothus, redbud, serviceberry, barberry, currant, gooseberry, blackberry, blueberry, huckleberry, salal, azalea, rhododendron, thimbleberry, salmonberry, and snowberry under that; and another layer of ferns, iris, violets, pyrolas, saxifrages, orchids, and hundreds of other wildflowers under that."

From northern California south to Santa Cruz, madrones flourish in the company of oaks again, including Oregon white oak. Here, madrones are most abundant on the dry soils of grassy balds just inland of the fogbound coast redwood forests. South of the redwood belt, this trickster tree crops up again in yet another ecological niche: it grows on cool, moist, north-facing slopes and along the bottoms of steep upper stream canyons in the high reaches of southern California's desert mountains as far south as Mount Palomar. From the wet north to arid south, the Pacific madrone's adaptations reflect the wide range of climatic conditions found along the western edge of the continent.

In his 1910 book, *Silva of California*, Professor Jepson writes of the "Council Madroña," a huge specimen in the Mattole River Valley in Humboldt County, California, that in 1902 measured seventy-five feet high, with a crown spread of ninety-nine feet and a girth of twenty-four feet! According to Jepson, this grand old tree, situated on a knoll on the mountainside with grassland all around, served as a meeting point for coastal and inland Indian tribes, a United Nations of sorts where people came to discuss intertribal matters and to arrange treaties. Today, the largest madrone on the Society of American Foresters' official big-tree record is a giant in Humboldt County, California, that stands ninety-six feet tall. Its trunk measures thirty-four feet around and its huge branches spread one hundred-thirteen feet from tip to tip. Perhaps this giant is Jepson's Council Madroña, a survivor like its species, embracing changing conditions to live on into another century.

White Sturgeon

Acipenser transmontanus

White STURGEON
(Acipenser transmontanus)

November 19th, 1805: We went four miles along the sandy beach to a small pine-tree, on which Captain Clark marked his name, with the year and day, and then returned to the foot of the hills, passing on the shore a sturgeon ten feet long, and several joints of the back bone of a whale, both of which seem to have been thrown ashore and foundered.

—Journal of Meriwether Lewis,
The History of the Lewis and Clark Expedition

RANGE: In the Pacific Ocean from the Gulf of Alaska south to
Monterey, California; large freshwater rivers along the coast
south to California's Sacramento River, inland as far as
western Montana

HABITAT: Feeds from ocean bottom and estuaries to far upriver;
spawns where rapids form in large rivers

NAME: White sturgeon are named for the light color of their
scutes, exterior bony plates; *sturgeon* comes from the Old
English name for these fish. *Acipenser* is Latin for "sturgeon"; *transmontanus,* Latin for "across" or "through" the
mountains.

SIZE: Adults reach twenty feet long, although five or six feet is
more common; the largest authenticated catch weighed
1,387 pounds

COLOR: Gray to olive-brown above, whitish below

NOTES: White sturgeon are North America's largest freshwater
fish.

WHEN THE LEWIS AND CLARK EXPEDITION reached the Pacific
coast in 1805, white sturgeon were so common in the Columbia
River and its estuary that the Clatsop Indians knew their English
name. "Sturgeon is good," a Clatsop commented to Captain Clark
in English, explaining that in winter he and his band walked the
beaches, foraging for storm-tossed sturgeon. "There is indeed,
every reason to suppose," Meriwether Lewis wrote in his journal,
"these Clatsops depend for their subsistence, during the winter,
chiefly on the fish thus casually thrown on the coast."

Sturgeon and humans go back a long ways. Their distinctive
horny scutes, or skeletal plates—these ancient fish possess external skeletons—are found in archaeological sites dating back

thousands of years. Sought after by Pacific Coast Indians, the white sturgeon were scorned as "nuisance fish" by later arrivals. By the late 1800s, however, immigrant Americans' tastes had changed—white sturgeon's delicate flesh and tasty caviar (eggs) had become fashionable food. So valuable, in fact, was the female's cargo of up to two hundred pounds of eggs that fishermen referred to it as "black gold." During the next few decades, white sturgeon were fished so heavily that they were nearly extirpated.

Today, white sturgeon spawn only in the three largest river basins of the Pacific Coast: the Sacramento/San Joaquin rivers of California, the Columbia River, and British Columbia's Fraser River. (Their smaller cousins, green sturgeon, are abundant seasonally in estuaries all along the northern Pacific coast.) The giant white sturgeon of old are no longer found, although medium-sized sturgeon are not uncommon. (Oregon and Washington laws require the release of white sturgeon longer than five feet to protect fish of breeding size.) The recovery of these long-lived fish has been limited by overfishing, water pollution, and especially by dams. Like salmon and some other fish, sturgeon are anadromous (literally, "running up rivers," in Greek). Although not as dependent on the open ocean as salmon, white sturgeon undertake long migrations, following the occurrence of food from river to estuary to ocean and back again. Lewis and Clark first encountered these giant fish on the Snake River in Idaho, hundreds of miles upstream from the ocean.

Dams now block all but the lower 159 miles of the Columbia River drainage, the entire upper Sacramento/San Joaquin River drainage, and the upper Fraser River. White sturgeon caught behind the dams are essentially landlocked, since fish ladders and other passage structures are not designed with these heavy bottom-dwellers in mind. Although white sturgeon may persist above dams for a long time—they can live as long as one hundred years—spawning conditions are limited. One landlocked population upstream of Shasta Dam on the Sacramento River has died out due to loss of spawning habitat. Below the dams, white sturgeon populations are stressed by pollution, commercial and sport fishing, and by the loss of estuaries, important feeding places. Still, over one million white sturgeon survive in the world's greatest sturgeon fishery, the Columbia River below Bonneville Dam.

Sturgeon are odd fish. They look like living fossils, with their bony exterior skeletal plates and toothless mouths. White sturgeon are bottom-feeders, like catfish, their heavy body and wide, sharklike noses perfectly adapted to swimming along just above the muddy or silty bottom. They feel and smell the water and bottom for food with their barbels, whiskerlike protrusions on their lower jaw. When a sturgeon senses something edible, it opens its mouth and ingests the food like a giant vacuum cleaner. Small adult white sturgeon eat a wide variety of foods, including invertebrates such as shrimp and mysids, larval mollusks, the larvae of aquatic insects, and copepods. Once a white sturgeon grows larger than about twenty inches, it turns to fish as a staple, both live and carrion.

Like salmon, white sturgeon do not feed randomly, but instead follow distinct migratory "paths" from freshwater to salt and back again, following the abundance of different foods. Unlike with salmon, we are only beginning to understand these cycles. In the Columbia River, where sturgeon populations have been the most intensely studied, adult white sturgeon move upstream out of the estuaries in fall, apparently to feed on the carcasses of spawned-out salmon and lamprey eels, and downstream in spring to feed on the spawning runs of various smaller fish, including an anadromous smelt called candlefish (these fish are named for their oil-rich flesh—Indians once dried and burned them as candles). In summer, adult white sturgeon congregate in the Columbia's large estuary.

White sturgeon grow to their enormous size slowly, depending on the food supply. They do not become sexually mature until they reach about twelve years of age and are five feet long. Females take longer—between fifteen and thirty-two years and at least six feet in length—because of the extra energy needed to produce the enormous quantity of eggs. Once mature, these great fish migrate upriver as early as February in the Sacramento River and as late as July in the Fraser. Mature white sturgeon spawn only about every three years, spending the intervening years feeding and recovering from the enormous effort required to reproduce.

Imagine their ponderous progress, the females heavy with pounds and pounds of "black gold," their small, dark gray eggs, the males carrying a load of milt. Unlike salmon, white sturgeon do not spawn in the shallows where all can see them; instead, perhaps to avoid predation, they pick the darkness of deep pools. Their spawning rituals are little known. Salmon die after spawning; sturgeon head back downriver to continue their lives.

I think of white sturgeon as the ghostly underwater elders of the Pacific Coast, rarely seen, swimming powerfully along on their ancient routes, connecting the saltwater with fresh as they traverse the cycles of their lives, eating and growing and spawning—living more years than most humans. Like redwood trees, white sturgeon accumulate a record of their aquatic decades in their flesh: when food was abundant and when not; when the water was clean, when polluted; the scars and snags in their sides tell stories of encounters with fishing nets and other hazards. They are like living epic poems, stories that include our heritage too. We need white sturgeon for the wisdom of their long lives, for the stories they carry that we do not yet understand.

SUMMER

SUMMER IS THE SEASON OF HALCYON WEATHER for much of the Pacific coast, when crowds of people turn out to enjoy the beaches, cliffs, and coastal waters. (Only the central coast may remain shrouded in fog, day after gray day.) Summer is also a time of almost unbelievable natural abundance: seabirds flock by the millions to island rookeries to breed, bat rays and sharks mass in estuaries to spawn, and marine invertebrates release literally trillions of eggs and sperm to float on the ocean currents (where most are eaten by larger creatures). On land, summer's abundance is exemplified in fruits, particularly berries: blackberries, dewberries, thimbleberries, salmonberries, huckleberries, raspberries, manzanita, and others.

Wherever islands or sea stacks punctuate the Pacific Coast, these isolated bits of terra firma attract dense, noisy aggregations of breeding seabirds: cormorants, puffins, gulls, shearwaters, murres, murrelets, and guillemots. Every square inch of island real estate is occupied, including sites that don't seem particularly suited to raising young: the narrowest of bare cliff ledges, simple scrapes in the soil of unshaded cliff tops, burrows in sheer slopes. For a few months, after seabirds fly in and court, these island rookeries come to deafening and fragrant life. Then, as soon as their offspring can swim or fly, the hordes depart for winter fishing grounds, leaving their nesting habitat as silent as an amusement park after closing time. The Farallon Islands west of San Francisco, just 211 acres in size, support one of the largest rookeries on the Pacific coast, with some three hundred thousand birds nesting on one island alone. That seabirds still nest on the Farallons at all is somewhat miraculous, since between 1849 and 1881 eggers harvested an estimated fourteen *million* eggs from the islands to feed San Francisco's booming Gold Rush population.

A different sort of breeding boom happens in the ocean in summer: spawning. As soon as water temperatures begin to rise in spring, many of the ocean's invertebrates, from red abalones to sea anemones, release staggering numbers of eggs and sperm into the water, trusting the currents to bring some together and start new lives. Most of this rich release of microscopic reproductive tissue is eaten by larger animals, but you can see some of the survivors growing in tide pools along the shore. Summer is the best time to go tide-pooling, but please just watch, and don't disturb the fascinating lives you find. Survival in the zone between the tides is difficult enough without adding the stress of human harassment.

Many saltwater fish spawn in summer as well; some, like sharks and bat rays, swim into the shallows of bays and estuaries to feed and reproduce. Take a kayak out on northern California's Humboldt Bay in August or walk the waterside trails at Elkhorn Slough National Estuarine Reserve near Monterey and scan the shallows for cruising sharks and bat rays.

From central California north, summer is berrying time. Although wild berries are most abundant in the wet forests of the northern coast, where half of the numerous shrub species sport edible berries, introduced Himalayan blackberries grow feral all along the coast as far south as Big Sur. These aggressive, thorny vines quickly produce formidable tangles wherever they take root, since the canes can grow sixty feet in a year. Look for blackberry patches in sheltered, unsprayed, sunny spots along the coast in August and pick your fill of succulent, sun-warmed berries.

From berries to breeding seabirds, summer is a fruitful time to explore the Pacific coast.

SOUTHERN SEA OTTER

Enhydra lutris nereis

SEA OTTER (*Enhydra lutris*)

The International Fur Seal Treaty, signed by the United States, England, Russia, and Japan in 1911, was almost too late. Fewer than fifty northern elephant seals remained, a handful of otters, and not enough Guadalupe and northern fur seals to even count. Otter pelts became so rare they fetched $1,700 at their peak. Stellar's sea lion was harvested, among other things, for its whiskers. They made nice pipe cleaners.

—Page Stegner and Frans Lanting,
Islands of the West: From Baja to Vancouver

RANGE: Formerly Baja California, Mexico, to perhaps southern Oregon, now Santa Cruz, Monterey, and San Luis Obispo counties and the Channel Islands National Park, California

HABITAT: Coastal waters within a mile of shore, mainly kelp beds

NAME: Southern sea otters are the southernmost subspecies of these ocean-dwelling weasel family members; *otter* comes from the Greek *hydra,* or "water snake." *Enhydra* is Greek for "in the water snake"; *lutris* is Latin for "otter"; *nereis* means "sea nymph" in Greek.

SIZE: Adults can reach six feet in length, including their heavy tail; males weigh as much as sixty pounds, females closer to forty

COLOR: Fur thick and dark brown; head grizzled with white or yellowish hairs

THERE IS A STORY IN AMERICAN HISTORY that we tell over and over again, in many different versions, as if we haven't learned it yet. It goes like this: An explorer (his name and nationality are not important) is shipwrecked on a remote coast—the exact location also does not matter. He dies, but his crew manages to survive the winter by killing and eating the curious, docile animals they find there. Come spring, the survivors patch together a boat from the wreckage, and sail back to their homeland, bearing pelts of the very animals that kept them fed and warm through the perilous season. The fur of the pelts (or the meat, or the shells, or the wood, or the feathers) is so precious that it sets off a rush to find more. Soon, ships of every sort are sailing the area, plundering this newfound resource. Eventually, the ships return with smaller and smaller cargoes, until finally the resource is gone. The hunters/loggers/fishermen lose their livelihood. And so the story ends.

In the case of the sea otter, the story is true. The explorer was the Dane Vitus Bering, the year 1741, and the location the Commander Islands of Alaska. Bering's crew indeed survived the winter by killing the newly discovered, docile sea otters. They ate sea otter meat, dressed in their pelts, made tents of the skins, and took seven hundred sea otter hides with them when they sailed home the following spring. The incredibly soft, lustrous, and dense fur—each pelt contains approximately one billion hairs—set off an immediate demand for more. Over the next 170 years millions of sea otters—no one knows the exact numbers—were killed along the Pacific Rim. By the time the International Fur Seal Treaty was signed in 1911, a few sea otters survived in the Aleutian Islands, but none of the playful animals had been sighted off the southern Pacific coast in decades.

Unlike most, this story may have an unexpectedly hopeful ending. On March 19, 1938, writes Gary Turbak in *Survivors in the Shadows,* rancher Howard Sharpe peered into a telescope on the front porch of his home above the rugged coast just south of Carmel, California, and spotted a bevy of strange animals frolicking in the kelp beds below. The creatures turned out to be none other than a colony of supposedly extinct southern sea otters. With protection, by 1994 the original group had grown to some two thousand animals living along the 220-mile stretch of the California coast from Monterey Bay south to San Luis Obispo. (The 1998 census, however, counted barely 1,800 sea otters, a dramatic drop. Biologists worry that water pollution may be killing the otters.) A colony was also transplanted to San Nicolas Island in the Channel Islands with the hopes that these gregarious animals will eventually repopulate the southern part of their range.

That anyone could have overlooked a colony of several hundred sea otters is more a tribute to the inaccessible nature of the Big Sur coast than to sea otters' habits. Like their freshwater cousins, river otters, sea otters are not shy and are amazingly acrobatic. In *Autumn Across America,* Edwin Way Teale describes his first view of Big Sur's otters: "Like a dark little log, it lay on its back, its feet rising stiffly in the air, floating amid the kelp. It was motionless, apparently sound asleep. Then we saw other little logs, four of them, five, six, seven." They spotted two otters playing in the crashing surf: "They rolled over and over, twining and intertwining, diving and being tossed aloft, floating on their back with head and feet in the air, swimming side by side with noses touching. . . . At times they spun in a fast sidewise roll. At other times they shot into view in curving, porpoiselike leaps."

These marine members of the weasel family are truly at home in the ocean. They hunt in the water, diving deep into kelp beds for sea urchins, abalones, crabs, clams, and mussels. After descending as deep as 250 feet and staying under for up to four minutes, a sea otter surfaces on its back and proceeds to eat its catch, using its furry chest as both kitchen counter and dining table. The otter balances its meal on its chest and carefully smashes the shell with a rock, then picks out the meat and eats it. When finished, the sea otter—still floating on its back—licks its paws, tosses away the inedible bits, and vigorously scrubs its furry "table." (A sea otter's dense fur is what allows it to survive a life in cold water; anything that fouls the fur, whether a meal or oil from an oil spill, destroys its insulating value.)

Sea otters court and mate in the water. Females give birth to their one, or rarely two, young while afloat, and nurse while floating on their backs as well. Like shearwaters and other pelagic birds that spend the majority of their lives at sea, sea otters even sleep in the water, lying on their backs with their uninsulated paws and noses out of the water, anchored in place with a strand of kelp to keep the waves from washing them away while they slumber.

Once given up for lost, southern sea otters are recovering slowly in the midst of controversy. Biologists applaud these predators for their consumption of sea urchins. Sea otters often eat so many purple sea urchins that their teeth and nails are stained purple. In the absence of predators like otters, purple sea urchins can "clearcut" whole giant kelp groves, their insatiable grazing denuding the once lush forests of the ocean bottom. Abalone fishermen, on the other hand, claim that otters' voracious eating habits are responsible for the decline in abalones. (Lacking fat, a sea otter consumes food equal to 25 percent of its body weight each day, up to twenty-five pounds of food, to keep itself warm in the cold ocean water.) Biologists counter that since abalone populations evolved with sea otter predation, it doesn't seem likely that the rebound of southern sea otters would alone be responsible for killing off the abalones. Are these playful weasels the saviors of kelp, swimming into town with white hats, or bad guys, competing with humans for a scarce resource? It isn't that simple, of course. Sea otters are simply part of a complicated web of lives that includes humans.

While waiting in line at a road construction site along Highway One on a recent summer day, my parents and I got out of the car to scan the kelp beds just offshore. On the rocks below us, black oystercatchers poked at mussels. Cormorants, pelicans, and gulls flew by just above the waves. About twenty yards offshore amidst the brown kelp fronds, I spotted a loglike floating silhouette: a sea otter, bobbing on its back in the swells. As I watched its bewhiskered face through my binoculars, the otter yawned, showing its sharp teeth, and stretched its forepaws upward as if just waking up. Then it rolled over as smoothly as any Olympic swimmer, and dove, disappearing beneath the surface. Just an otter, taking care of otter business.

CABEZON

Scorpaenichthys marmoratus

There isn't any symbolism. The sea is the sea. The old man is an old man. The boy is a boy and the fish is a fish.

—Ernest Hemingway,
Letter, September 13, 1952,
to the critic Bernard Berenson,
on *The Old Man and the Sea*

Range: Sitka, Alaska, south to Punta Breojos, Baja California, Mexico

Habitat: Rocky tide pools to reefs as deep as 250 feet

Name: *Cabezon,* "big head," in Spanish, describes the shape of these fishes' bodies, largest at the head end. *Scorpaenichthys,* Latin for "scorpion fish," is misleading—these fish resemble scorpion fish, but are actually sculpins; *marmoratus,* "marbled" in Latin, describes their mottled coloration.

Size: Adults to three feet, three inches long (females are larger than males), with a blunt snout, helmetlike head, and large, winglike fins set behind the gills

Color: Mottled in red to olive-green to brown on a light ground; can change color to blend into its background

PEER INTO A TIDE POOL with a cobble bottom, looking carefully at each "rock," and you may notice a flutter of gills: what looks like an inanimate stone is actually a fish. These rocklike fish are cabezon, denizens of rocky bottoms from the lower intertidal zone to offshore kelp beds. Like octopuses, cabezon are predators that lurk on the bottom, waiting for lunch: other fish, crabs, abalones—anything smaller and mobile. Also like octopuses, these strange-looking fish can change their color to blend in with their background, allowing them to "hide" in the open. But cabezon take the camouflage strategy one step further: their mottled color pattern mimics the colonists on an actual rock, making the fish look as if they harbor patches of seaweed, sponge, and other creatures.

A cabezon on the hunt hangs out near the bottom, its splotchy patterned skin looking just like a rock colonized by sedentary lives. When it spots toothsome prey, a cabezon rushes forward with powerful thrusts of its oversized fins and tail, and opens its large mouth wide to swallow the meal whole. Cabezon find their way into tide pools with the incoming tides, and ride the outgoing flow back offshore into the underwater kelp forests. The retreating sea sometimes leaves small cabezon behind in tide pools.

In kelp forests, these big-headed fish are bottom-dwellers as well, skulking along in pursuit of their prey like wolverines hunting a terrestrial forest floor. Cabezon are just one of many fish that inhabit the underwater groves for all or part of their lives: more than 150 species of fish frequent kelp forests. As with terrestrial forests, the inhabitants avoid competition by partitioning the space and the food resources. They live at different levels of the seaweed forest, from "ground level" at the ocean bottom to the upper canopy near the water's surface, and they feed on different foods: some are predators, some gleaners, munching epiphytic lives from the kelp itself; some graze on kelp fronds, and some harvest parasites from other fish.

Besides cabezon, the bottom-dwelling predatory fish include lingcod, rays, halibut, painted greenling, sculpins, island kelpfish, and scorpionfish. These fish inhabit the forest "floor," staying within a few feet of the ocean bottom. Of these bottom-dwellers, some, including lingcod, rays, and halibut, rarely leave the "ground," dwelling in crevices or half-buried on the ocean bottom itself, while others swim along just above the ocean floor. Although larger fish generally hunt larger prey, and smaller fish smaller prey, there are exceptions. Pacific halibut, for instance, the largest of the bottom-dwellers, grow to immense sizes—lengths of over eight feet and weights up to eight hundred pounds. But these enormous fish dine on small creatures: marine worms, sand dollars, shrimps, crabs, and the siphon tips of clams.

Other species of fish dominate the mid-canopy level of the seaweed forests. Giant sea bass weighing up to four hundred pounds cruise between the kelp "trunks" on the hunt for smaller fish and invertebrates, along with up-to-six-foot-long leopard sharks and more modest sized predatory fish, including pile perch, rubberlip seaperch, California sheephead, kelp bass, and garibaldi. Schools of Pacific sardines flash between the kelp trunks like silvery showers of snow, slurping up floating plankton.

Still other fish species make the upper canopy their home. There, near the water's surface and exposed to the view of aerial predators such as pelicans, gulls, and terns, most of these fish camouflage themselves to look like floating plant parts or detritus. Giant kelpfish, for example, have evolved an elongated shape, olive-brown coloring, and a swaying swimming motion that makes them look just like kelp leaf blades. Slender tubesnouts, named for the shape of their narrow snouts, hide among the tangled blades near the water's surface, resembling floating detritus.

A whole other group of fish, including señoritas, topsmelt, blacksmith, and halfmoon, swim the kelp forest from top to bottom, grazing on the kelp, eating plankton, or gleaning small organisms from the seaweed or from other fishes' bodies. Señoritas, thin fish up to ten inches long and bright yellow with black tails, glean parasites directly from the skin of other fish. Far from camouflaging themselves to avoid becoming lunch, señoritas may use their bright pigments to advertise their "services." Other fishes seldom prey on these cleaners, and in fact may line up to be scoured.

When a cabezon ventures shoreward with the tide and is trapped in a tide pool by the retreating waters, it hunkers down on the bottom and adjusts its coloring to blend in, escaping notice by looking just like an algae-mottled rock. Not all fish found in tide pools, however, blend in. Garibaldi, bright reddish-orange fish dotted with luminous blue spots in their younger years, positively shout to be noticed. No surprise, then, that juvenile garibaldi, or ocean goldfish, are the most frequently noticed fish in tide pools along the southern Pacific coast. (Adult garibaldi spend most of their lives in kelp forests.) Named for the bright red shirts worn by Giuseppe Garibaldi and other Italian patriots in the late 1800s, their vivid color allows them to be easily spotted from land. Goldfish Point, off La Jolla, California, is named for the garibaldi frequently sighted offshore.

There is no symbolism to these fish, as Hemingway wrote. A cabezon is just a cabezon; a garibaldi, a garibaldi. But what wonderful stories they tell us about life in the ocean!

Cobra Lily

Darlingtonia californica

Cobra Lily or
California Pitcher Plant
(Darlingtonia californica)

Just by looking at this strange plant you will know right away that there is something weird about it, and you're right—it eats insects.
—James Luther Davis,
A Seasonal Guide to the Natural Year:
Oregon, Washington, British Columbia

RANGE: Extremely restricted, from north of Florence, Oregon, to northern California

HABITAT: Sphagnum bogs along the coast, often on serpentine rocks

NAME: Cobra lily is neither lily nor snake; it is named for its leaves' resemblance to cobra heads swaying on long necks. *Darlingtonia* honors William Darlington, a Pennsylvania Quaker who practiced medicine and botany in the early nineteenth century; *californica* is for California, where the plant was first collected.

SIZE: Leaves up to three feet tall, tube-shaped and hooded; flowers about two inches across, singly, on stalks slightly taller than leaves

COLOR: Leaf tubes bright green but turning yellow, red-purple, and brown as they age; flower petals dark purple-red; sepals yellow-green

AS A YOUNGSTER, I didn't always pay attention to the natural history lessons that my parents taught during our family vacations. But I did have an appetite for the bizarre. One summer, on a trip along the Oregon coast, we stopped behind coastal dunes at a dense grove of western red cedar and Sitka spruce. Down a path, a boardwalk led into a bog; there grew a patch of the strangest plants I'd ever seen. Hundreds of pale-green, hooded tubes stuck out of the shallow water, cheek by jowl, like a forest of photosynthetic periscopes. What caught my adolescent attention, though, was the odd plants' diet: they ate insects.

The cobra lily is the perfect plant to captivate any adolescent with an appetite for gore. It belongs to the pitcher plant family, one of the few plant groups whose members are carnivorous—they trap and eat insects. Unlike other carnivores, which roam about in search of prey, carnivorous plants are at a distinct disadvantage: they are rooted in place. Thus, they must lure prey in, then trap and kill it. Some carnivorous plants are active trappers: these may, for instance, use sensitive hairs to trigger folded leaves that snap shut on the hapless prey. Others are passive: luring the insect into a pool of enticing but deadly fluid within the plant.

The cobra lily is among the latter. At the base of the plant's tubular leaves is a pool of liquid where trapped insects drown. The plant is named for the shape of the leaves, tubes that rise up and curve over at the top into a cowl-like hood that looks something like a cobra about to strike. Two leaflike bracts that contain nectar glands hang down from the underside of the hood, resembling a broad, V-shaped snake tongue hanging out of an open "mouth," the opening that leads into the tube.

The hungry insect sips from nectaries in the bracts and then, enticed by the smell of more nectar emanating from the tube, crawls into the opening. Once in, there is no way out. If it tries to crawl out, the insect slips down the waxy skin inside the tube, sliding into an area of sharp, downward-pointing hairs lining the lower part of the tube. The hairs allow downward, but not upward passage. An insect that tries to fly out becomes confused by the light transmitted through clear patches in the top of the hood. It flies toward the light, hits the top of the hood, bounces off, flies toward the light again, and so on, never finding the real opening on the side. The exhausted insect finally drops into the pool at the base of the tube and drowns. Other pitcher plants digest their food by secreting enzymes into the pool; cobra lilies let bacteria do the decomposition, then absorb the remaining proteins.

Why would a plant that can manufacture its own food using chlorophyll and sunlight expend the extra energy needed to grow a complicated mechanism to catch insects? In order to grow, plants need a source of free nitrogen, a crucial element that they normally acquire from the soil. But cobra lily and other insect-eating plants live in bogs, environments so acidic that nitrogen isn't available. To remedy this deficiency, they have turned to obtaining their nitrogen from the proteins in insects.

There is one drawback to eating nectar-loving insects: pollination. If you are an insect-pollinated plant, like cobra lily, how do you lure insect pollinators for your own flowers without, so to speak, eating the arthropod that pollinates you? The cobra lily does it by having its flowers, purplish-red affairs, grow atop stalks taller than its deadly leaves, and by having them broadcast a different scent, thus attracting a different kind of insect. Cobra lily flowers open in spring, and are probably pollinated by flies, among the earliest pollinators to emerge.

The cobra lily is the only member of the pitcher plant family on the Pacific coast, and, in fact, it is the only member of its genus, *Darlingtonia*. This queer plant is rare as well, confined to a small area of the coast from northern California through central Oregon by its adaptation to the specialized habitat of bogs: even along this wet part of the coast, acidic bogs are not a common habitat. (And they are becoming rarer, dredged and converted to the sunken fields of cranberry farms.)

Far from the acidic bogs on the fog-shrouded Pacific coast, a cemetery in West Chester, Pennsylvania, holds the grave of William Darlington, the nineteenth-century Quaker doctor and botanist. His gravestone is decorated with a carved likeness of a cobra lily, the peculiar insect-eating plant that bears his name.

Xerces Blue Butterfly

Glaucopsyche xerces

Xerces Blue Butterfly
(Glaucopsyc
xerces)

← Tree Lupine
(Lupinus arborens)

Pick out just one form of life, besides people, and care about it. Forget the California condor. It's better if it's a little musquash, guib or buzzing thingamajig that nobody else thinks about. Adopt it. Do your best to make sure that it gets the space, air, water and food it needs. Those are what everything needs. Just make sure that your little musquash, guib or thingamajig gets them because if they do, the condor will be okay too.

—John Cody,
Tijuana River National Estuarine
Research Reserve Visitor Center

Former Range: Upper San Francisco Peninsula, from about North Beach to the Presidio and south along the coast to the Lake Merced District

Former Habitat: Coastal sand dunes

Name: Xerces blue's common name, like that of many insects, is simply a translation of its scientific name, "blue butterfly that lives in dry places." *Glaucopsyche* is Greek for "bluish-gray butterfly"; *xerces*, "dweller in xeric places" in Greek, alludes to their sand-dune habitat.

Size: Butterfly phase one and one-eighth to one and one-quarter inches across, wingtip to wingtip; caterpillar phase to about an inch long

Color: Male butterflies lilac-blue above, females bluish-brown above, both gray-brown below with white spots and long, silvery hairs; caterpillar pale green with yellow markings, covered with white hair; chrysalis gray-green

Notes: Xerces blue butterflies are extinct.

You can't see the Xerces blue butterfly alive today. The dunes where it once lived on the seaward edge of the San Francisco Peninsula have disappeared under the city, or are overgrown with exotic vegetation. The last known colony of the Xerces blue lost out to the U.S. Army in the war effort when the Presidio was expanded in 1943, giving this small, silvery butterfly the dubious distinction of being the first butterfly species to be extirpated by human activity.

Why tell the story of a vanished butterfly? Because it illustrates what happens when an organism is adapted to a naturally limited habitat and that habitat becomes valuable for human uses: if no one is paying attention and speaking up for the little folks, the organism loses. Once it is gone, its story goes, robbing us of the knowledge to be gained from its life. Each species, writes biologist E. O. Wilson in *The Diversity of Life,* is important for reasons that we may not yet know, ones that may touch us intimately. "Signals abound that the loss of life's diversity endangers not just the body but the spirit," he writes. If we are not careful, the story of the Xerces blue may foretell the future of coast-dwelling plant and animal species as human development obliterates more and more wild habitat.

What we do know about the Xerces blue is sketchy but intriguing. Like many butterfly species, Xerces blues had very specific tastes. In fact, their lives were tied to two particular sand-dune plants, yellow tree lupine and deerweed, both members of the pea family. These small, fog-colored butterflies emerged from their chrysalis in March or April and chased after each other over the dunes with reproduction on their minds. After mating, females laid their tiny, turban-shaped eggs on one of their two host plants. The flattened caterpillars that hatched spent their days crawling around on the leaves of tree lupine or deerweed, munching on buds, flowers, and tender new pea-pod-like fruits.

Like most butterfly caterpillars, Xerces blues were camouflaged to avoid attracting the notice of predatory insects or hungry birds. In the Xerces blue's case, the succulent caterpillars were colored like their host plant and even grew a cover of whitish hairs, mimicking the plant perfectly. A larva ate and grew until the time came to spin its camouflaged chrysalis near the base of the plant. Many species of blue butterflies have "noisy" chrysalises: while pupating the chrysalis makes faint sounds by flexing its body and rubbing its membranes together. Lepidopterists (people who study butterflies) think the noise repels parasites and other small predators.

Yellow tree lupine, one of Xerces blues' two host plants, tells its own interesting life story. Growing up to nine feet tall and equally wide, these shrubby lupines flourish on seaside sand dunes and sandy slopes near the ocean along the entire California coast. (In fact, they have been introduced in Oregon and Washington to stabilize loose dunes.) Yellow tree lupines dot open dunes like miniature trees; their dense crown of hairy, compound leaves provides shade and thermal cover for small dune residents. The covering of white hairs on their skin buffers this hardy shrub from the desertlike conditions of life in the dunes, including wide day-to-night temperature swings and long periods of summer and fall drought. The hairs provide shade, slow down evaporation from the plant's tissues, and even collect dew for the plant to drink: moisture in the air condenses on the hairs at night.

From May through September, yellow tree lupine's spikes of fragrant, yellow, pealike flowers hum with the activity of bees and other small nectar feeders. Despite their name—*lupine* comes from the Latin *lupinus*, or "wolflike," for the belief that these plants robbed the soil of nutrients—yellow tree lupine, like most lupines, houses nitrogen-fixing bacteria in nodules in its roots. Nitrogen produced by the bacteria enriches the plant tissue, which in turn fertilizes the impoverished dune soil when the plant decays.

Sand dunes are not an abundant habitat on the largely rocky Pacific coast. Some river mouths on the southern California coast end in dunes; dunes line the southern edge of Monterey Bay, and parts of the San Francisco Peninsula. Oregon boasts only one dune field, but it is the coast's largest, a forty-mile-long swath of dunes running from Coos Bay to north of Florence. Washington's only dunes line the slender reach of the Long Beach Peninsula. British Columbia's coast lacks dunes entirely. These scattered coastal dune areas share one characteristic: isolation. Each rises like a desert island from the surrounding landscape, and like an island, each has evolved unique plant and animal communities. Nipomo Dunes, south of Pismo Beach, California, for instance, shelters at least eighteen species of endemic plants. On summer weekends, it is also the playground for literally thousands of four-wheel-drive vehicles.

And therein lies the rub: dunes are coastal real estate, and coastal real estate is a hot commodity for human habitation and recreation. Sand dunes have been "stabilized" with introduced exotic vegetation such as European beach grass, South African ice plant, and Scottish gorse, all of which alter dune habitat and outcompete native species. Dunes have been paved over, built upon, or loved to death by all-terrain vehicles and trampling human feet. Hence the extinction of the Xerces blue, and the endangerment of a host of other creatures that depend on coastal dunes, including California least terns, snowy plovers, and the Nipomo mesa lupine, a cousin to the plants that once hosted Xerces blues.

Blue butterflies, in particular, have taken to dunes, evolving specific species and subspecies for each sand-dune area. Five of California's federally listed endangered species are blue butterflies, three of those are restricted to tiny areas of remnant dunes. The El Segundo blue, for instance, hangs on in three hundred acres of dunes west of Los Angeles Airport that remain undeveloped only because their open space is necessary for overflying aircraft.

In an ironic and perhaps hopeful coda to the extinction of the Xerces blue butterfly at the hands of the military, another species, Smith's blue, survives in part because the U.S. Army maintained a butterfly reserve in the undeveloped dunes at Fort Ord, near Monterey. Perhaps, after all, we are learning to share.

Bat Ray

Myliobatis californica

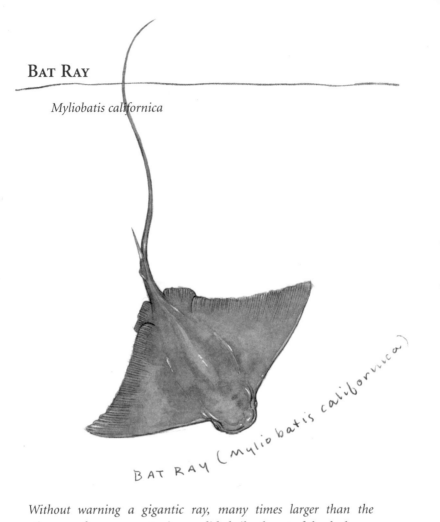

BAT RAY (Myliobatis californica)

Without warning a gigantic ray, many times larger than the stingrays of common experience, glided silently out of the darkness, beneath my dangling feet, and away into the depths on the other side. It was gone in seconds, a circular shadow, seeming to blanket the whole bottom. I was thunderstruck.

—E. O. Wilson, *Naturalist*

Range: Offshore from Oregon south to the Sea of Cortez (Gulf of California), Mexico

Habitat: In shallow bays and over sandy bottoms offshore to a depth of 150 feet, including kelp beds

Name: Bat rays are related to both stingrays and sharks; when they flap their wide, winglike fins, they appear to fly through the water like bats. *Myliobatis*, "millstone-toothed ray" in Greek, describes the fish's stout grinding teeth; *californica*, "of California," refers to where it was first described.

Size: Up to six feet wide with a slender, whiplike tail up to two and one-half feet long

Color: Slate gray, dull olive-green, or brownish above, creamy-white below

ONCE I TOUCHED A BAT RAY as it glided near me, its wide, winglike fins propelling it smoothly through shallow water. The ray's body brushed my fingers, its skin surprisingly warm and velvety soft, the thrust of its fins sinuous and powerful. As quickly as it came, the ray was gone, gliding swiftly away along the bottom. For hours afterward though, my fingers could still feel the bat ray's blood-heat warmth and its plush skin.

Bat rays may fly gracefully through the water on what look like wings, but they are fish. In fact, they are close cousins to sharks, sharing sharks' use of flexible cartilage rather than rigid bone for their skeletons, sharks' strong jaws and ferocious-looking teeth, and other structural features. But unlike most sharks, rays are flattened, perfectly suited for life near the bottom of the ocean.

A bat ray's body looks much like its mammalian namesake, with a rounded head and two big, protuberant eyes up top, and a pair of wide, flattened, triangular-shaped fins attached—again, batlike—from head to tail. Those huge, winglike fins are a highly modified form of the side-attached pectoral fins of most other fish. They are the bat ray's most obvious modification for bottom-dwelling life, but not the only one. Most fish breathe through gills placed on the sides of their head, for instance, but when bat rays evolved their flattened body, the gills ended up below, where sediment would choke them. Rays thus *inhale* through spiracles atop their flattened head, and *exhale* through their gills. Their eyes have moved up top, too, so that bat rays can see even when lying flat on the bottom. Even the tail has lost its fishlike look, instead modified into a whiplike appendage that conceals one or more stinging spines (modified fins) at its base.

Rays swim by flapping their pectoral fins, seeming to fly through the water, instead of undulating their tail in a side-to-side motion like other fish. Their unique locomotion, powered by those winglike fins, also serves to excavate their dinner: oysters, clams, marine worms, and other creatures that burrow into sandy bottoms. A hunting bat ray "hovers" just above the bottom sediments, beating its fins in place. The wide surface area of the fins creates so much downward pressure that loose sediments are swept away, exposing burrowing creatures. In some cases, the wings' downward pressure may even act like a plumber's helper, popping burrowing animals right out of their holes! The ray gobbles up the exposed food and crushes it, shells and all, with its blunt teeth.

A bat ray defends itself from larger predators with slender, dagger-shaped spines at the base of its whiplike tail. When whipped into the flesh of an unwary attacker, the spine cuts a wicked gash and injects a neurotoxic venom strong enough to affect animals as large as humans.

Bat rays spend most of their lives away from shore, but in summer, they and some of their small shark cousins cruise into bays and estuaries to spawn. A female ray doesn't deposit a cloud of eggs for external fertilization as most other fish do. Instead, after mating as most terrestrial animals do, she carries the young until they are large enough to fend for themselves. The young are born tail first, with their wings wrapped around their bodies. Their venomous spines are rubbery and covered with a sheath to protect their mother. Within days, however, the spine hardens and is ready for use.

Bat rays share their ocean-bottom habitat with other rays, including the Pacific electric ray, named for its literally stunning electric charge, and with several species of small sharks.

I say that I touched a bat ray, but the ray touched me as well. Until I felt its warm, soft skin, I hadn't thought of rays as kin, as some*one*—not some*thing*—I cared about more than as a collection of interesting facts. The bat ray's body heat warmed my heart, the way the sound of a kitten's purring does. It spoke to me, as one life to another.

LIGHT-FOOTED CLAPPER RAIL

Rallus longirostris levipes

Clapper RAIL
(Rallus longirostris)

My generation has lost the belief that our children's lives will be better than our own. We know that our sons and daughters will inherit an earth made shabbier and less abundant.

—Sharman Apt Russell,
Kill the Cowboy: A Battle of Mythology in the New West

RANGE: Historically, along the Pacific coast from Santa Barbara, California, south to Bahía San Quintín, Baja California, Mexico

HABITAT: Cordgrass meadows of coastal salt marshes

NAME: Clapper rails are named for the sound of their calls; *light-footed* refers to either this bird's stealthy gait or its light-colored feet. *Rallus,* "thin" in Latin, describes their frontal profile; *longirostris,* "long-beaked" is for the bird's lengthy beak; *levipes* means "light" in Latin.

SIZE: Adult birds 14 to 16$^1/_2$ inches long, beak to tail tip, slightly smaller than a crow, and flattened side to side

COLOR: Marsh-colored; back mottled in gray, brown, black, and buff, chest tawny, white streaks on the flanks, white patch under tail, feet and legs pale; eggs pale yellow to olive, blotched with brown and gray

VOICE: A startlingly loud "kek, kek, kek," given ten or so times

FOR A BIRDWATCHER to count a bird on their life list, they usually have to see it. But some birds are so secretive, so difficult to catch sight of, that you can count them if you hear their voice. So it is with rails. These rarely glimpsed birds spend their lives in the mucky tangle of marshes, slipping stealthily through the dense thickets of marsh grass—unless they hear a competitor. Then they let loose with a loud, harsh cackle, like the sudden clapping of cupped hands. The call says "This is my space!" Thus, the trick to "seeing" a rail in a marsh is to stand on solid ground at the edge and clap your hands loudly, then listen for a response.

Light-footed clapper rails spend their entire lives in tidal grasslands, moving in and out with the tide, skulking through the dense grasses on longish legs, their big feet keeping them from sinking in the ooze. They are so narrow that they can pass through the tightly packed plant stems without disturbing them, thus rendering their progress invisible to predators. (The rail's width, in fact, gave rise to the expression "skinny as a rail.") These marsh-dwellers are most active at dusk and dawn, stalking cordgrass and pickleweed flats with their tails constantly flicking. They probe the mud with their long beak for worms, clams, marine snails, and other invertebrates, or snatch crabs, insects, fish, and small animals such as mice on the run.

These secretive birds only live in marshes where cordgrass grows. Cordgrass, for its part, only grows in tidal salt marshes. With slender leaves that stretch as tall as three feet from creeping stems rooted in the salty muck, cordgrass has evolved sophisticated adaptations to its half-aquatic, half-terrestrial, highly saline environment. Hollow stems transport oxygen to its submerged roots. Special glands allow the plant to secrete excess salt on the outside of its leaves. Nitrogen-fixing cyanobacteria live in nodules in the roots, feeding the plant their homegrown fertilizer. And cordgrass produces its food through an alternate form of photosynthesis commonly found in desert plants and plants subject to drought stress.

Like the underwater eelgrass meadows, thick stands of emergent cordgrass are richly productive. Their underground stems trap detritus and build a layer of fertile soil, home to burrowing marine worms, snails, clams, and innumerable smaller lives. This bounty in turn attracts small fish and crabs, which themselves feed larger animals, including migratory birds. Despite the rich food sources, few animals live in cordgrass meadows: the grasses offer scanty cover from the weather and from predators, the water level moves up and down, and the ground is only exposed at low tide. For clapper rails, however, these estuarine grasslands are the perfect home.

Light-footed clapper rails have evolved an innovative nest

architecture to deal with the problems of tidal flooding and lack of cover. They build a cuplike nest of grasses and sedges in a clump of cordgrass or pickleweed near the high-tide line, then anchor their construction in place with a plaited line of grass fibers. For shade and protection from the keen vision of predators, they weave a canopy of grasses and other fibers overhead. Inside this snug, semi-floating home, the female clapper rail lays seven to eleven eggs, which both parents incubate for about three weeks. The downy young spend most of their time near the nest until they fledge and can fly, nine to ten weeks after hatching.

This bird's dependence on cordgrass marshes is at once its strength and weakness. Although John James Audubon reported finding a hundred clapper rail nests a day in the marshes of the Atlantic coast, the rocky Pacific coast has never boasted an abundance of cordgrass marsh habitat. What did exist has been diked, drained, filled, developed, or polluted, especially along the southern Pacific coast. In 1974, the California Department of Fish and Game estimated that only five hundred to seven hundred of these shy birds remained in perhaps a dozen marshes. But even where protected, light-footed clapper rails have continued to decline because of nest predation by nonnative red foxes and black rats. (Ironically, coyotes, often thought of as "vermin," may be the answer to controlling the introduced red foxes. Coyotes outcompete the much smaller foxes, and they rarely prey on ground-nesting birds such as clapper rails.) By 1986, only 143 pairs of light-footed clapper rails survived.

Light-footed clapper rails are just one of dozens of species—including humans—affected by the decimation of estuaries on the southern Pacific coast. These meeting places of fresh and saltwater are nurseries for many marine animals that we eat, including fish, shrimp, lobsters, and crabs. Estuaries produce nutrients that serve to fertilize the ocean, trap pollutants, and provide valuable open space in densely developed landscapes. In short, they are vital to the health of the whole Pacific coast.

There are signs of hope for estuaries, if not for light-footed clapper rails. On a recent trip along the Pacific coast, my parents and I walked through a restored cordgrass and pickleweed marsh at the Tijuana National Estuarine Research Reserve, a stretch of wild marsh between the crowded, often-polluted cities of San Diego and Tijuana. Snowy egrets stalked for fish, long-billed dowitchers probed for invertebrates, and light-footed clapper rails—we were told, we didn't see them—hunted the cordgrass meadows, apparently oblivious of the press of humanity.

We can still choose whether or not the earth our children will inherit will be shabbier and less abundant. If we can restore estuaries and light-footed clapper rails, we'll have made a big step in the right direction.

ORCA

Skaana
Orcinus orca

Male KILLER WHALE
(Orcinus orca)

Female

As I leaned wearily into the oars my ears pricked to underwater sounds, high-pitched squeals and clicks I half recognized before the water erupted into bubbles around our boat and we began to spin in a slow whirlpool. "Orcas!" I shouted. "Everywhere!" I leaned over, plunging my hands into the roiling bubbles.

—Brenda Peterson,
Nature and Other Mothers:
Personal Stories of Women and the Body of Earth

Range: In the Pacific Ocean, from northern Alaska south to the Equator; in the Atlantic, from pack ice south to the Gulf of Mexico

Habitat: Upper layers of coastal waters, sometimes moves into large rivers

Name: The common name, *orca*, comes from the Latin species name, which means "whale"; *orcinus* means "whalelike" in Latin. The Haida Indians of the far northwest coast call these cetaceans *skaana*, the "chiefs of the world beneath the sea."

Size: Adults up to thirty-two feet long, with tall dorsal fins (to six feet in males, three in females); males weigh up to ten tons; calves average seven feet long at birth and weigh four hundred pounds

Color: Glossy black with white undersides, a broad white "eyebrow" over each eye, and a distinctive grayish, saddle-shaped mark behind dorsal fin that identifies individuals

Notes: Orcas are also called killer whales, but they are actually the largest members of the dolphin family.

In the past three decades, the public image of orcas has undergone an amazing transformation in public image, from "killer whales" despised for their wolf-pack-like hunting style and voracious appetite, to "orcas" beloved as totem animals of the Pacific Northwest and starring in popular movies. Once so scorned that U.S. Air Force pilots used them as targets for strafing practice, orcas now attract whale-watchers by the thousands. What caused our image of these big dolphins to change? In the 1960s, a number of orcas were captured for display at places like San Diego's Sea World. Seen up close, these "killer whales" charmed viewers with their engaging behavior and amazed researchers with their intelligence and sophisticated language.

Like any animals, including humans, the real orcas defy simplistic labels: they are neither solely cold-blooded killers nor charming entertainers. Orcas are cetaceans, members of the order that includes whales and dolphins. Like all cetaceans, orcas possess large brains, are intelligent and adaptable, and use echolocation to navigate and hunt. Orcas' brains, in fact, are four times the size of human brains by weight, and largely comprised of cerebral cortex, the part that handles, among other things, language. It was what researchers discovered about the orca's social behavior and complex vocalizations that changed their public image.

In the late 1970s, in response to concerns about the number of orcas being captured for marine parks, researchers Kenneth Balcomb and John K. B. Ford began studying orcas, Balcomb in the San Juan Islands of Puget Sound and Ford in the area of Vancouver Island. The two researchers' findings changed our perception not only of these predatory dolphins, but of the complexity and richness of nonhuman animal behavior.

Balcomb, now director of the Center for Whale Research, focused on the social structure of the orcas in his area. By photographing thousands of orcas and comparing the shapes of their dorsal fins and saddle markings, he learned to identify individuals and discovered that orca society is matrilineal and family centered. Orca calves are born singly, and stay within a few body lengths of their mother for their first year. Even after that, they don't stray far, spending their entire lives swimming with their mother and their siblings. Orca females mate first in their teens, and bear young only every four to six years. Orcas past reproductive age live on with their family group, acting the role, biologists believe, of grandparents.

Each orca family belongs to a "pod," a larger group of up to fifty animals. Orcas hunt in pods, defend other pod members, socialize and loaf with their pods, and travel in pods. In summer and early fall, two or more orca pods gather in a superpod, possibly to give male orcas a chance to mate with females outside their genetic group.

In 1978, Ford, now Director of Research at the Vancouver Aquarium, began what he imagined as a two-year study of the communication of orcas off British Columbia. Using a hydrophone, tape recordings, and computer analysis, Ford found that orcas make as many as sixty-two separate sounds, including high-pitched whistles, squeals, howls, and screams, combining these in a dozen different types of discrete "phrases" or calls. (Cetaceans are known for their vocalizations.) What amazed Ford was that orca pods in different geographic areas speak radically different dialects. Such pods would have as much difficulty understanding each other as, say, an Alabaman speaking "pure Southern" and a Maine farmer speaking "down east." (Orca language is different from the clicking sounds orcas use in echolocation.)

Orcas use their calls—which can be heard underwater up to two miles away—to maintain contact with other pod members and to coordinate group activities, such as hunting. (Coyotes and wolves do much the same thing with their "yip-howl" call.) Orca language is learned, not innate: orca calves acquire their language from their mother and other family members. Twenty years after the beginning of Ford's two-year research project, he is still so fascinated with orca "speech" that he has started ORCA-FM, a twenty-four-hour radio station, to broadcast the underwater chatter from Robson Bight, off Vancouver Island, one of the world's busiest orca intersections.

Pacific Northwest orca pods fall into one of two types: resident pods, spending their summers in the same offshore territory, and transient pods, which have no fixed summer territory. Orcas in these pods swim as far as nine hundred miles up and down the coast over the summer months. (With a top speed of seven knots, orcas can cover sixty to one hundred miles of ocean a day.) The two kinds of pods don't interact much. Transients, Ford discovered, speak a totally different language than residents, with far fewer calls; they are often silent. Further, all the transient pods along the two-thousand-mile-long Pacific Coast share at least one call type, leading Ford to speculate that these wandering orcas may have evolved from one community. Resident pods and transient pods even eat different diets: residents feed primarily on salmon, herring, halibut, and other fish; transient pods hunt a wide variety of prey, including pinnipeds (seals, sea lions, and other marine furbearers) and other dolphins and whales.

Orcas come by their "cold-blooded killer" reputation honestly. Agile, strong, and armed with mouthfuls of sharp teeth, orcas are the top predators in the oceans. Like wolves, they hunt in family groups and often rip into their prey before it is killed. Pod members hunt cooperatively, surrounding their prey, and, swimming closer and closer, literally driving it into the mouths of their fellow pod members. Orca pods "herd" fish by swimming in ever-tightening circles around a school, while blowing out a "net" of silvery air bubbles that traps the confused fish. Weighing in at several tons, orcas eat a lot: a medium-sized orca in captivity may consume one hundred pounds of fish a day (an orca beached on Vancouver Island had several full-sized Dall's porpoises in its gullet).

Orca or killer whale: two sides of the same reality—very like humans when you think about it.

GEODUCK CLAM

Panopea generosa

Geoduck
(Panopea generosa)

Shell from GEODUCK

Omnia exteris. [Let it all hang out.]

—Motto,
The Evergreen State College,
Olympia, Washington

Range: Southern Alaska to Scammon's Lagoon, Baja California, Mexico, most common in the northern part of its range

Habitat: Burrows in sandy mud from intertidal flats to three hundred feet deep in the ocean bottom

Name: *Geoduck,* pronounced "gooey-duck," is from a Chinook Indian phrase meaning "dig deeply." *Panopea* comes from the Greek for "all-opening," referring to this clam's shell, which cannot close; *generosa* from "generous," for the animal's large size.

Size: Adult shells oblong, to ten inches in length, the siphon (the clam's long "neck") may stretch over two feet; weight, as much as twenty pounds, more commonly five or so

Color: Shell yellowish to grayish-white; skin reddish-brown and wrinkled, like elephant skin

Notes: Geoducks are the largest burrowing clam and may live up to 140 years.

WHEN PACIFIC COAST RESIDENTS go clam-digging, they don't usually dig for geoducks, even though just one of these behemoths can yield half a dozen clam "steaks." Digging geoducks requires too much muscle and time. These heavy, long-lived clams inhabit burrows as deep as four feet in the muddy sand of the intertidal to subtidal zone.

When disturbed, a geoduck quickly retracts its long, elephant-trunk-like neck or siphon, making it seem as if it is digging deeper. Actually, these clams are weak diggers, and although a geoduck can pull its siphon down to near its shell, it cannot fit inside: the shell is too small; the animal simply too large. If you do reach the creature, don't grasp the tip of the siphon and pull;

the siphon is not strong enough to lift the heavy clam and will only break off. Edward F. Ricketts and others in *Between Pacific Tides* tell the story of a noted conchologist who spent a long time digging out a geoduck with the aid of two other men. Afterward, the conchologist "referred to it feelingly as 'a truly noble bivalve.'"

Despite their heroic size and extraordinary longevity—geoducks can live longer than human beings—these clams live typically clammy lives. Born in spring on the chance meeting of the hordes of eggs and sperm released on the ocean currents by their parents, the minute, mobile, larval geoducks are as unlike the familiar adult clams as caterpillars are butterflies. For the first seven months of their life, geoduck larvae drift along near the water's surface with the legions of plankton, a microscopic and near-microscopic community of tiny creatures, including algae, clam and bivalve larvae, and the young of many other marine animals. Geoduck larvae catch minute particles of food and metamorphose through three distinct phases over their first summer, finally reaching the twin-shelled adult form.

As miniature adults, geoducks sink to the bottom and attach themselves by super-strong woven cords called byassal threads. The larva may move several times in the next several months, using its byassal threads as a sort of parasail to float to a new location along the bottom. But by the end of its first year, the inch-or-so-long geoduck has dug the burrow where it will remain for the rest of its life. (All bivalves go through a similar life cycle, from free-swimming or drifting larva to settled, shell-dwelling adult.)

Once settled, geoducks turn to a life of filter-feeding. They ingest phytoplankton—microscopic plants—and other edible debris by extending their siphon upward through the mud to the surface of the ocean bottom. Powerful body muscles suck water down the siphon and through the clam's digestive system. The clam filters out the food particles and jets the wastewater, plus inedible debris, back up the tube to be expelled. Geoducks grow slowly, taking ten years to reach six inches in shell length. They spawn after their third spring, releasing clouds of eggs or sperm into the currents between March and June, earlier in the south, later in the north.

In their larval stage, geoducks are food for nearly every larger creature that eats the microscopic plankton "soup" of the oceans, from minute tube worms to giant whales. Once they have settled into their burrows, these big clams are much more difficult prey. The tender tips of their siphons are "grazed" by sea stars, crabs, bat rays, and bottom-dwelling fish such as halibut, but only humans impact their populations seriously. Millions of pounds of geoducks—three million from Washington State alone—are excavated each year by divers using water hoses like giant Water Piks to dig out the individual clams. Most are shipped live, on ice, directly to Asian markets, where a five-pound geoduck may fetch $100.

Geoduck shells are filled to overflowing with the animal's fleshy body, but other clams have enough space in their shells that smaller animals take up residence there. Gaper or horse clams, for instance, house pea crabs, miniature crustaceans, in a small hollow space between their mantle and shell. The crabs, less than an inch across and shaped like their name, apparently find their way into the mantle cavity as larvae, attracted by fragrances released by the clam. Pea crabs spend their adult lives in the protected space inside the clam, feeding on diatoms and other minute food brought in by the water currents generated by their host. Although some researchers consider the tiny crabs freeloaders or even parasites, others posit that the crabs act as sanitarians, keeping the clam's home clean and disease-free.

Geoducks are not lovely creatures: out of water, their flaccid, rubbery siphons protrude a foot or more from their oblong, paired shells, looking almost obscene. But they are beautifully adapted to their lives, dug deep under the tidelands, grazing on the minute tidbits carried by the ocean currents.

GIANT GREEN ANEMONE

Anthopleura xanthogrammica

Giant Green
ANEMONE
(Anthopleura
xanthogrammica)

With the tip of a forefinger I touched the orifice of one of the green sea anemones. With surprising suddenness all the petals of the tentacles turned inward, closing on my finger.
—Edwin Way Teale, *Autumn Across America*

RANGE: From Unalaska Island, Alaska, south along the Pacific
coast to Panama

HABITAT: Rocks, seawalls, pilings, tide pools, and on the bottoms of bays, from above the low-tide line to water fifty feet
deep

NAME: Giant green anemones are named for their size and
color; *anemone,* from the Greek word for "wind," refers to
this animal's resemblance to the flowers of anemones,
members of the buttercup family. *Anthopleura,* "side-
flower" in Greek, refers to the tentacles' resemblance to
petals; *xanthogrammica,* from the Greek for "yellow" and
"writing," apparently refers to the origin of the anemone's
green color.

SIZE: Disk up to ten inches across with numerous inch-long tentacles, column up to a foot high; these are among the
world's largest anemones

COLOR: Usually pale to bright green; albino when growing in
dim light

NOTES: Giant green anemones have lived as long as sixty-nine
years in captivity

ONE INCREDIBLY FINE SUMMER AFTERNOON when I lived in
Washington, my friend Terry and I sneaked away from work to go
sea kayaking. Out on Nisqually Inlet, the sun warmed our backs
and the water was glassy calm. After paddling a while, we rested,
drifting near the shore. I looked over the side into the clear water,
and there on the sandy bottom just beneath the kayak was a large,
startlingly green sea anemone. As I watched, its flowerlike disk
convulsed, the center drawing in and the tentacles disappearing
into the mouth. A moment later, it "burped," ejecting a piece of
shell; the tentacles reappeared and the disk rearranged itself back
into a placid underwater blossom.

Sea anemones got their name because of their deceptively

lovely, flowerlike appearance. But the name of their phylum, Cnidaria, literally "nettlelike creatures," is a better clue to their character. These anemones are not plants at all, but carnivorous animals, closely related to jellyfish, hydroids, and corals. In the adult stage of their lives, sea anemones are sedentary or nearly so, attached to the ocean bottom or to some solid object underwater by the suction-cup-like disk at the bottom of the fleshy cylinder that comprises most of their body.

The top of a sea anemone's column is what appears flowerlike: the flat oral disk with a slitlike mouth at its center, surrounded by several rows of petal-like tentacles. The gently waving "petals," however, are actually potent armaments. Each tentacle is tipped by a nematocyst, a capsule that explodes on contact, expelling a sticky, threadlike dart studded with venomous barbs into the flesh of whatever touched it. The barbs carry a neurotoxin powerful enough to stun or kill small animals such as crabs, fish, sea urchins, and shellfish. Although the barbs aren't large enough to pierce human skin, the poison may cause a tingling or sticky sensation.

Sea anemones "hunt" by sitting patiently, their seemingly innocuous tentacles open wide. When a smaller creature such as a sea urchin carelessly walks across the anemone or a fish brushes the tentacles, the nematocysts release their stinging barbs, stunning the prey. The tentacles quickly fold inward like a flower closing with the night, bearing the food to the anemone's mouth. Once inside, the meaty parts are digested in the animal's baglike stomach, and the inedible shell and bones are heaved back out of the mouth slit with a very human burping motion.

Unlike most sea anemones, which cluster in colonies of dozens or hundreds, giant green anemones are most often solitary creatures. But near dense aggregations of food, such as mussel and sea urchin beds, these huge anemones may crowd together to benefit from the foraging of predatory sea stars (starfish). A sea star strolling into an urchin bed, for instance, provokes an underwater stampede. As the spiny creatures try to escape their many-armed predator, some invariably rush off into the tentacles of giant green anemones. Also, sea stars are messy eaters; anemones may snag chunks of meat and shell they drop.

Giant green anemones get their startling coloration from other lives within their own tissues. When these anemones live where there is sufficient light, minute algae—either bright green unicellular critters called zoochlorellae or yellow-brown dinoflagellates called zooxanthellae—take up residence in the tissue lining the anemone's digestive tract. Both types of algae possess chlorophyll and synthesize their own food from sunlight. Some of the food they produce leaks through their cell walls and into their host, similar to what happens with lichens, where a food-producing algae feeds the fungus within whose tissues it resides. What is not clear is whether the anemone-algae relationship is similar to that of the fungus and algae that make up lichens, where the non-photosynthesizing fungus, which cannot survive on its own, captures and essentially enslaves free-living, photo-synthesizing algae as a food source. Like the species of algae in lichens, the algae of sea anemones can and do survive on their own. Giant green anemones apparently can exist without their algal partners, although they grow more slowly. Zooxanthellae have a similar relationship with coral, except that for these reef-farming ocean creatures, the food supply produced by the tiny algae is crucial—without it, the coral die. Scientists have recently discovered that coral "bleaching," the loss of color and subsequent death of coral in ocean reefs, happens when the zooxanthellae are killed by overly warm ocean water such as that in recent El Niño episodes.

Despite their stinging tentacles, sea anemones are vulnerable to predators. Some nudibranchs, brightly colored sluglike animals, graze the tips of the tentacles and ingest the nematocysts, which lodge—in perfect working order—at the ends of the nudibranch's tubercles, soft "spines" protruding from their backs. The nudibranchs use the borrowed nematocysts in their own defense.

Other predators simply crawl or saunter up to an anemone's succulent column and begin to feed. Wentletrap snails, tiny, long-spiraled snails, secrete a violet-colored toxin that acts as an anesthetic, numbing the tissues before they begin chewing. Sea spiders, tiny crustaceans that look like minute, scrawny crabs, are not so subtle: they sink their sharp proboscis into the anemone's soft flesh and suck its juices until dislodged.

"Whenever I go down into this magical zone of the low water of the spring tides," wrote Rachel Carson in *The Edge of the Sea*, "I look for the most delicately beautiful of all the shore's inhabitants—flowers that are not plant but animal, blooming on the threshold of the deeper sea." Strange flowers, indeed: they live underwater, sting with their petals, house algae within their tissues, and eat meat.

Marbled Murrelet

Brachyramphus marmoratus

Marbled MURRELET
(Brachyramphus marmoratus)

One of the strangest birds that a person can expect to find in moist coastal forests is a seagoing bird known as the marbled murrelet. This species, which spends most of its life out on the Pacific Ocean, nests in the tops of tall trees up to several miles from the sea.
—Allan A. Schoenherr,
A Natural History of California

RANGE: Aleutian Islands to central California, also Siberian coast

HABITAT: Feeds and winters in protected, nearshore waters, including in passages between islands, bays, and estuaries; nests in old-growth forests within twenty miles of coasts or on the ground in mountains above treeline

NAME: Marbled murrelets are named for their mottled breeding plumage and their small size. *Brachyramphus* means "short beak" in Greek; *marmoratus* is "marbled" in Latin.

SIZE: Adult birds eight inches long, beak to tail tip, slightly smaller than a robin, but much plumper

COLOR: In summer, marbled rust-brown all over; in winter, white underneath and black to gray above; eggs cryptically colored, lichen-green to pale yellow and dotted with various colors

NOTES: Marbled murrelets are listed as threatened under the Endangered Species Act.

IMAGINE CLIMBING A TREE twelve stories high and discovering, on a lichen-crusted branch near the top, a bird nest. But not just any bird's nest, the nest of a little-known seabird whose nesting habitat was the last to be discovered of all the North American bird species. That is exactly what happened in 1974 in Big Basin Redwoods State Park in California: a tree trimmer working 140 feet off the ground in a Douglas fir encountered the nest of a marbled murrelet. Ornithologists had speculated for years about where these small, plump seabirds nested. Although they spend most of their lives on the ocean, observers as early as Joseph Grinnell in the 1920s reported hearing marbled murrelets call at dawn and dusk in forested areas miles inland. But a nest had never been located. (Scientists later learned that a marbled murrelet nest had been discovered in 1961 on Russia's Siberian coast.)

Marbled murrelets are members of the alcid family of pelagic, or ocean-dwelling, birds, along with guillemots, puffins, auklets, murres, and the extinct great auk. Like penguins, alcids are diving birds, able to descend to great depths and swim with speed and agility by "flying" underwater with their wings. Both alcids and penguins have webbed feet, thick layers of insulating fat, large preening glands for waterproofing their plumage, salt glands to excrete excess salt from the seawater they ingest, and narrow, flipperlike wings. Despite these many similarities, penguins and alcids are not closely related. They are instead a case of convergent evolution: different organisms adopting similar features to adapt to similar conditions. Besides their range—penguins live in the Southern Hemisphere, alcids in the Northern—the two groups of birds are separated by one significant difference: alcids (with the exception of the great auk) can fly; penguins cannot. In optimizing themselves for deeper diving, ornithologists believe, penguins grew too heavy to fly. Alcids stayed smaller and thus retained flight, although just barely—they must beat their wings rapidly to keep their plump bodies aloft—while settling for fewer diving skills.

Alcids spend the majority of their lives in saltwater, often far from shore, coming ashore only to nest. Most, including common murres, tufted puffins, and pigeon guillemots, nest in noisy and odoriferous colonies on shore cliffs or islands inaccessible to terrestrial predators. Murrelets, however, have chosen different habitat. Both the marbled murrelet and its northern cousin, Kittliz's murrelet, nest singly: Kittliz's nests on the ground on arctic tundra or above treeline in the mountains, marbled murrelets nest on the limbs of the tallest trees in old-growth forests or, north of where such forests grow, on the ground as Kittliz's does. Both murrelets—perhaps because of their unique nesting habitat—are also the only alcids to change their plumage for the summer, shedding their drab gray and white for camouflaging mottled brown.

Once ornithologists knew where to look for marbled murrelet nests, they still proved hard to find. The nests don't stand out: the female simply lays one cryptically colored egg on a mat of lichen or moss on a tree limb or in a hole in the trunk high in the canopy. The downy chick hatches out camouflaged to blend into its background; the parent birds spend the daylight hours at sea miles away, diving for fish, returning only at dusk. Ornithologists eventually learned to locate nesting sites by watching and listening for the parents flying out of the forest at dawn and back at dusk.

Like all other alcids, marbled murrelets are at home on and under the water. Unlike most, they spend their time near the coast, usually in water less than one hundred feet deep. Marbled murrelets are accomplished fishermen, diving after schools of small fish, including sand lance, sea perch, and herring. They also catch small crustaceans, including certain types of shrimp and amphipods. Beating their wings swiftly and steering with their webbed feet, these plump divers are so quick and agile that they can cut an individual fish out of a school and herd it away to catch and store in their bill.

Fishing the shallows puts marbled murrelets in particular peril from oil spills and human fishermen. Thousands of these birds became fouled with oil and died after the Exxon *Valdez* spill in Prince William Sound, Alaska, in 1989. These and other alcids also become entangled and perish in salmon gill nets. The state of Washington considers diving-bird mortality in regulating coastal salmon gillnetters.

Their unique nesting habitat has pitched marbled murrelets headlong into controversy. Like the spotted owl, various salamander species, red-backed and other voles, and other lives, these cryptically colored seabirds need undisturbed forests of big, old trees in order to survive. The supply of such habitat has shrunk dramatically in the past three decades as human appetites for timber products have grown. In 1992, marbled murrelets were listed as a threatened species under the federal Endangered Species Act. Listing these plump, little-known seabirds doesn't guarantee their survival, but it does mean that their welfare must be considered in resource management decisions.

Imagine felling a huge tree in an old-growth forest, then finding in the litter of limbs of the shattered tree crown a stunned marbled murrelet parent and the fragments of an egg. It's like Humpty Dumpty falling off the wall and breaking into pieces. Once we've cut the trees, try as we might, we can't put the pieces of old-growth forests back together again.

FALL

FALL IS A TOPSY-TURVY SEASON along the Pacific coast: it begins more summery than summer and ends as wet as spring. Early fall days on the central and northern coast bring some of that area's warmest and driest weather, the best days all year for heading for the beach. When the weather finally turns, though, it brings a welcome change: rain. The cool, damp weather works its way down the coast from the north, and by mid- or late November has reached the land of surf and sunshine in southern California and northern Baja California. Central and southern landscapes, tinder-dry after months of drought, green up almost immediately, exactly as if spring had arrived.

The change in the weather comes from a change in the path of the jet streams, the high-speed winds that circle the Northern Hemisphere from west to east. In summer, these storm-bearing winds pass over the northern part of the North American continent, carrying storms across Alaska and Canada. In winter, the jets move south, bringing their moisture-bearing cyclones with them. A storm sucks up moisture as it crosses the Pacific. When this soggy air mass hits land, it must rise to pass over the coastal mountain ranges. As it rises, the air in a storm cools and its moisture condenses, turning to fog and rain.

As with spring, the changing weather of autumn signals changes for animals and plants as well. Migratory creatures, for instance, head for more clement climes before winter catches them. "Fall" migration really spans many months, however. Shorebirds that nest on arctic tundra start south in midsummer; gray whales are still steaming south for calving lagoons in December. The restless mood strikes creatures of all sorts, from monarch butterflies to brown pelicans. Not all migration is north to south, either; as the fall rains green up the dry hills of the southern coast, some inland residents, including Costa's hummingbirds, head for the now verdant coast.

Change prevails in other ways too. In the ocean, the tiny planktonic generation of some marine lives settles down in fall, rooting to a firm substrate to weather the winter storms. The hydra stage of moon jellyfish, for instance, attach themselves to the undersides of rocks and float in shallow water. Autumn weather signals some species of salmon to swim inland from the ocean to spawn in coastal rivers and streams. The adults' dying bodies sustain all manner of creatures, from bald eagles and grizzly bears to river otters and deer mice. Salmon thus bring nutrients from the ocean to nurture terrestrial ecosystems.

Inland, fall rains sprout a bounty of mushrooms, the spore-bearing, reproductive bodies of some fungi, from damp forest soils. The rain forests of the Pacific Northwest are a mushroom-hunter's paradise, boasting more species of edible fungi than anywhere else in North America, from the delicate, apricot-scented chantrelle to massive puffballs. Look for mushrooms in any moist coastal forest, but beware of poisonous lookalikes: *never* eat a mushroom unless you have identified it positively as an edible species.

From spring green in the south to winterlike storms in the north, autumn is an exciting time on the Pacific Coast, a time to gather in the last harvest and watch for harbingers of change, for signs of transition as the days grow shorter and the sun more distant.

Harford's Greedy Isopod

Cirolana harfordi

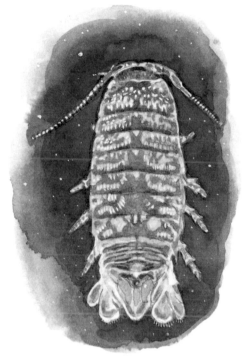

Hartford's Greedy
ISOPOD
(Cirolana harfordi)

To me, the sea is like a person—like a child that I've known a long time. It sounds crazy, I know, but when I swim in the sea I talk to it. I never feel alone when I'm out there.

—Gertrude Ederle,
the first woman to swim the English Channel,
New York Post

RANGE: British Columbia to Ensenada, Baja California
HABITAT: Under rocks on sandy bottoms, in mussel beds
between the high- and low-tide lines, and on kelp holdfasts
in shallow waters
NAME: Harford's greedy isopods are named for their discoverer,
and their eating habits; *isopod*, "equal-footed" in Greek,
refers to this crustacean's seven pairs of similar legs. The
meaning of *Cirolana* is obscure; *harfordi* is the Latinization
of "Harford," presumably the name of this creature's discoverer.
SIZE: Up to three-quarters of an inch long and one-quarter inch
wide, with a flattened body consisting of a head, seven segments, and a fan-shaped "tail"
COLOR: Tan, grayish, brown, or blackish, sometimes two-toned
or speckled, varies by the background color of its habitat

WHO COULD RESIST a creature named Harford's greedy isopod?
Especially since these miniature crustaceans are so aptly named:
they descend on their food—usually decaying fish carcasses—in
hordes. Like starving guests at some Roman banquet, they rip
into the meal, gorging themselves until not a scrap remains. A
swarm of these tiny marine scavengers can strip a fish carcass
bare in a matter of hours.

As with most scavengers, whether as large as California con-
dors or as small as desert darkling beetles, the Harford's greedy
isopod's eating habits are an adaptation to the sporadic occurrence of their food. Sensitive antennae and chemoreceptors on
their feet allow these less-than-inch-long aquatic creatures to

detect the delectable flavors of rotting food many yards away. When Harford's greedy isopods locate a meal, they tank up. After eating as much as their small systems can handle, they retire under a submerged rock or into a crevice to digest their feast in a leisurely fashion. It may be a month or more before food comes their way again.

Although Harford's greedy isopods are common, and their eating habits well documented, little is know about the remainder of their lives. When they are not gorging themselves at a decaying feast, the tiny crustaceans spend their days tucked away underwater, beneath rocks on sandy bottoms, squeezed between the crowded shells in a mussel bed or in crannies between the "roots" of a kelp. Thus concealed, they are safe from predatory shallow-water fish such as sculpins.

Harford's greedy isopods do emerge from their shelters long enough to mate. Although their mating ceremonies are not known, they may be similar to those of distant freshwater relatives, fairy and tadpole shrimp. Cued by environmental signals, these crustaceans mate with fervor: pairs of males and females grasp each other and twirl in aquatic ballets that may last for hours. Although we don't know their exact mating rituals, we do know that fertile female Harford's greedy isopods carry their young (several to many dozen) in a special brood pouch until the miniature isopods are large enough to fend for themselves.

Scientists believe that this habit of carrying the young internally is one of the traits that has helped isopods and their relatives, amphipods (including beach hoppers and sand fleas), to move out of the ocean and colonize land. One of the most successful terrestrial isopods is the familiar pillbug or roly-poly of gardens and compost piles, so named for its habit of curling up into a tight ball with its armored back outward. Pillbugs haven't left their aquatic ancestry entirely, however; they are found only in damp places, such as under rocks or logs.

A far less common isopod, the Socorro isopod, found in only

one warm spring near Socorro, New Mexico, demonstrates this tiny animal's extreme adaptability. When these swimming pill-bugs were first discovered, biologists were stumped about how they arrived at the springs, surrounded by miles of waterless creosote bush desert. Turns out that Socorro isopods are the descendants of a species of isopod common in the shallow seas that covered the Southwest 130 million years ago. As the continent moved, and the seas retreated, replaced by desert, the little isopods moved upstream out of the saltwater and eventually into isolated freshwater warm springs such as those at Socorro.

Harford's greedy isopod is not the only marine isopod to live a scavenging existence. Other isopods also act as recyclers, feeding on dead tissues and liberating their nutrients for new life. The western sea roach, named for its flattened, cockroachlike appearance and its nocturnal habits, scours rocks and jetties near and above the high-tide line for decaying animal food. Sea roaches spend the daylight hours squeezed into crevices, and emerge at night in crowds to scavenge. These inch-long isopods change color diurnally, turning darker in the day and lighter at night, and spend more time out of the water than most marine isopods.

If you have ever felt a tingling or itching sensation while wading barefoot in a tide pool, you may have been nipped by hungry Harford's greedy isopods. Biologists speculate that some of the substances that we apply to our skins, including suntan lotion and perfume, taste like decaying fish to these tiny crustaceans. Just as colors appear different through different eyes, so apparently are smells and tastes perceived differently by different sensory organs. It's a good reminder that the impressions we leave are not always what we intend.

CALIFORNIA LEAST TERN

Golondrinita marina
Sterna antillarum browni

Least TERN
(Sterna antillarum)

With its forked tail fanned and tiny tapered wings backpedaling against the wind, the smallest of our southern California terns stalls in midair to scrutinize an anchovy or silversides in the water below. The bird plunges into the water from high above to capture [its] prey.

—Peter Steinhart, *California's Wild Heritage*

RANGE: San Francisco Bay south to Baja California

HABITAT: White sand beaches and alkali flats

NAME: California least terns are named for their size—least terns are the smallest North American terns—and the state where this subspecies breeds. *Tern* comes from the Old Norse (*taerne*) and Swedish (*tarna*) names for the birds. "Little sea swallow," their Spanish name, describes their size, pointed wings, forked tail, and buoyant, butterfly-like flight. *Sterna* is the Latinized version of "taerne"; *antillarum* refers to the Caribbean Antilles, where the species was first described; *browni* commemorates the person who described this subspecies.

SIZE: Eight to nine and one-half inches long—smaller than a robin—with a twenty-inch wingspan; eggs just one and two-fifths inches long

COLOR: Mostly white, with leading edge of wings black; in breeding plumage, a black cap with a white forehead; in fall, the black cap recedes to a tonsure

---

BEHIND A TALL CHAIN-LINK FENCE just a few yards from Highway One where it follows the ocean's edge around the Los Angeles Basin lies Bolsa Chica estuary—a slice of open water behind a slender sand spit, dense patches of saltgrass and pickleweed, and salt-crusted flats dotted with birds. Houses crowd the edges of this small marsh, traffic roars by on six lanes of highway, airplanes thunder overhead. Bolsa Chica ("tiny pocket" in Spanish) is just a dot of open space in the crowded basin, but its fecund acres harbor millions of lives, including California least terns, the smallest and most graceful of North America's gull family, and one of the most endangered.

Least terns spend their summers in the Northern Hemisphere, their winters as far south as Brazil. After their return in April and May, these *golondrinitas* congregate with dozens or hundreds of their kind to nest on white sand beaches along the coast or alkali flats of estuaries and inland rivers. Unfortunately for California least terns, their nesting habitat is also the chosen playground for millions of humans intent on sunbathing, surfing, jet-skiing, jogging, or playing volleyball. In the conflict for space, the small, ground-nesting birds have lost out. They once nested abundantly on the beaches of central and southern California: in 1909, for instance, observers counted a colony of six hundred on just one beach in San Diego. In 1994, the California Fish and Game Department estimated that less than three thousand California least terns remained in the whole state.

California least tern colonies survive only where their nesting areas are protected from human intrusion and predation by pet cats and introduced red foxes. This usually means behind fencing. There, they go about the business of their lives, apparently undisturbed by whizzing Frisbees or staring bird-watchers. Male least terns court females with what ornithologists call a "fish flight": a male darts over the colony of perched terns, carrying a small fish in his bill and loudly announcing his intentions in a harsh voice. Female terns take flight and chase the hopeful male. He and his bevy of followers flutter and turn and glide as if dancing in the air. The various females eventually tire and drop out of the aerial dance, but for the female that persists, the reward is a mate and a slice of ground for nesting.

The two birds land and continue their dance on terra firma, him strutting before her, wagging his tail, flicking his wings, and shaking the fish so that it shimmers in the sun, her bending low and quivering her wings like a chick begging to be fed. After their ritual, he feeds her the fish and they copulate. The pair then builds a simple nest: one bird sits on the ground and kicks its feet backward while rotating on its breast. Two days later, the female lays two or three tiny eggs in the shallow depression. (Hence the need for fencing or other protection, or the well-camouflaged eggs may be crushed, unnoticed, by beachgoers.)

Both parents incubate the eggs and feed the young. Because the nests are out in the open, unsheltered, the parents must not only protect their offspring from predators, but also provide thermal protection until the chicks gain enough feather covering and body mass to withstand heat and cold. During the daytime, the parents spread their wings wide for shade; at night, they gather their charges under their breast for warmth. In extreme heat, the parents resort to evaporative cooling: one flies to nearby water, wets its breast feathers, returns to the nest, and shakes the water on the young to cool them down.

The parent that isn't incubating the eggs and brooding the growing chicks is flying a constant food relay. Least terns fish in shallow water, flying along with quick wingbeats while looking down at the water's surface for the glimmer that means food—small fish like anchovies, topsmelt, and grunion, as well as shrimp. When a least tern spots a flash of food, it pauses in the air, hovering briefly, then dives into the water headfirst. If it is successful, the bird emerges with fish or shrimp in its beak and flies homeward.

When the chicks are around four weeks old, the parents take them to a nearby estuary where they can learn to feed themselves. In calm water with abundant food, the young terns gain weight and experience for the long trip south to their wintering grounds. They may not return until they are ready to breed, two years later.

That least terns have survived at all is something of a miracle. Before the coastal development boom of this century nearly eliminated their nesting habitat, these elegant *golondrinitas* weathered wholesale slaughter in the name of fashion. After the Civil War, no fashionable lady's hat was complete without bird plumes or skins. So pervasive was the craze that in 1886, Frank Chapman, the American Museum of Natural History's ornithologist, went bird-watching along the streets of Manhattan and spotted forty species of native birds—dead, their wings or whole skins arranged on ladies' hats. By then, least and gull-billed terns were in particular demand for their natty white and black plumage. Hunters killed as many as one hundred thousand of these birds a season—up to twelve hundred birds a day in parts of their range. The slaughter stopped after 1913, when, on the edge of extinction, they were finally protected.

Watching through the chain-link fence at Bolsa Chica as a California least tern hovered, its elegant pointed wings holding it in place against the strong sea wind, then dropped like a stone into the water, emerging with a small fish in its beak, I wondered when we humans would be able to tear down our fences and invite nature back into our lives.

ECCENTRIC SAND DOLLAR

Dendraster excentricus

*Eccentric
SAND DOLLAR
(Dendraster.
excentricus)*

Every time I pick it up to study a detail, a few [sand] grains slip out. . . . This particular dollar has continued to yield since I found it on the Kenya coast in March of '91, and the manner in which it imparts clues serves as a reminder of the way science works. A mere three and a half inches in diameter, and less than a half an inch thick at its apex, it yields a volume scarcely suggested by its dimensions. It was still yielding when I wrote the last page of this book.

—Delta Willis, The Sand Dollar and the Slide Rule

RANGE: Southeastern Alaska to Baja California, Mexico

HABITAT: Sandy bottoms of sheltered bays and open coasts, from the low-tide line to 130 feet deep

NAME: Sand dollars are named for the resemblance of their skeleton to a silver dollar. *Dendraster,* literally "tree-star" in Greek, is for their five-parted, star-shaped symmetry; *excentricus,* "eccentric" or "off-center," describes their star pattern.

SIZE: Adults to three inches wide and one-quarter inch deep; flattened disks

COLOR: Light lavender-gray, reddish-brown, or dark purple-black; skeleton bleaches white

NOTES: Sand dollars can live as long as thirteen years, but six to ten is more common.

ON MY WRITING DESK sits a sand dollar that I picked up from a beach in northern Oregon. Its near-perfect disk and its intriguing shape invite closer inspection. Many times I've marveled at its symmetric design, the perfect curve of its upper side, and the delicate engraving that resembles a five-pointed star. But the sand dollar I hold is only a skeleton, a lifeless remnant of the animal that built and inhabited this calcareous form.

Sand dollars are echinoderms, in the group of invertebrates named for their spiny skins (*echino* is Greek for "spiny," *derm* means "skin"). Along with their relatives, sea stars and brittle stars, sea urchins, and sea cucumbers, sand dollars are characterized by five-parted, radially symmetric bodies, skeletons of calcareous plates, and spines embedded in the skin. (Soft, fleshy sea cucumbers seem unlikely members of the group, but they are radially symmetric when viewed from one end, and sport internal plates and spines.)

The familiar sand dollar skeletons found on the beach are bleached and smooth, but the living creatures are variously colored and, like sea urchins, covered with a dense felt of spines. Unlike sea urchins, however, sand dollars possess short and soft spines, more like turgid, silky hairs. Nor are these defensive weapons, as sand dollars simply "walk," burrow, and gather food with their spines. The tiny spines move in rhythmic waves, along with the animal's tube feet, to displace sand so that a sand dollar can burrow or move along.

Looking at a sand dollar skeleton, with its flattened profile, dome-shaped upper side, and flat lower side with central hole, it is hard to imagine the animal that lives here. Indeed, sand dollars are odd creatures, adapted to a life on the sandy sea bottom.

The star-shaped design on the top of a sand dollar shell is comprised of minute pores, each holding a tiny foot shaped like a short, flexible tube. The animal pulls in water through pores in the center of the star, and funnels it through an internal system of canals to a hollow bulb at the base of each tube foot. When the bulb is empty, it contracts and the tube foot lengthens; when it is full and relaxes, the tube foot is withdrawn. Using this water-vascular system, the sand dollar moves its hundreds of suction-cup-tipped tube feet in rhythmic motions to quickly shift sand.

In quiet water or in very rough currents, sand dollars lie horizontally on the surface or partly buried in the sand; where currents are light or moderate, they sit vertically, half of their body buried, like ranks of coins standing on edge. When lying prone, sand dollars feed on detritus found between the grains of sand—pieces of algae, microscopic organisms, and other organic matter. As the water currents move sand over the dollar, bits of food fall between the spines on the upper side and are pushed by the movement of the cilia, fine hairs covering the animal's skin, down to the lower margin and thence to the underside of the sand dollar, where more cilia wash the food to the central mouth. Inside are five grinding teeth, held in a circular arrangement by an intricate system of muscles and calcareous plates called an Aristotle's Lantern for its resemblance to an ancient Greek lantern.

Sand dollars in the vertical position are suspension-feeders, snagging bits of floating food out of the stream of water flowing by them. (A sand dollar can capture food anywhere on its body.) Either way that sand dollars feed, they ingest lots of sand along with their meals, hence the grains that leak from their dried skeletons. Juvenile sand dollars smaller than about an inch across actively eat large sand grains, which they store in a special "weight belt" in their lower intestines and use as ballast to hold their position in the shifting sand.

Like many marine invertebrates, sand dollars reproduce by releasing hordes of eggs and sperm in late spring or early summer to float on the ocean currents and contact each other by chance. Fertilized eggs develop into free-swimming, planktonic larvae that look nothing like their parents. Larvae that are not eaten by the hordes of plankton eaters metamorphose into minute, sand-dollar-shaped adults after a few weeks and drift until they find a sandy bottom to settle on, usually in their first autumn. Larger sand dollars, sea stars, crabs, and other bottom-dwellers such as flounders, halibut, and bat rays all eat smaller sand dollars. Only a tiny percentage, perhaps 1 percent, of the three hundred thousand eggs exuded by one female each year survive to reach a large size.

Sand dollars vie for living space with other inhabitants of sandy bottoms, including sea pansies, colonial animals distantly related to sponges. Sand dollars may live in dense enough colonies (up to six hundred per square yard) that they exclude sea pansies, but the presence of the tightly packed dollars also benefits the colonial creatures, since sand dollar beds act as barriers to sea stars, one of the sea pansies' main predators. (One of the sea pansies' defenses against predators is to light up, emitting an eerie blue phosphorescence.)

When I pick up the dried skeleton of the sand dollar on my desk, I am astonished by the stories that I know it contains. No matter how intricate and beautiful the shell, it is only the husk of the living creature that created it.

Salicornia virginica

Pickleweed
(Salicornia virginica)

About the oddest of seaside plants is Salicornia, all stem and branches. . . . There are no leaves, no flowers in the ordinary sense of the word. . . . Some plants, like some people, are like that, you say, purely practical, careless about beauty, thinking only of material results; and yet every autumn the sober green of the Salicornia's homely stems and branches is transfigured to a vivid red or crimson, and the salt marshes where it grows are sheeted with such richness of color. . . .

—Charles Francis Saunders,
Western Wildflowers and Their Stories

RANGE: Along the Pacific coast, from Alaska to Baja California, Mexico

HABITAT: Salt marshes and saline soils on beaches, from the mid-tidal zone to the high-tide line

NAME: Pickleweed is named for the resemblance of its fat, succulent stem joints to miniature pickles. *Salicornia*, "salt-horned" in Greek, commemorates this plant's saline habitat and the hornlike appearance of the branches; *virginica*, "of Virginia," in Greek, is puzzling, since the species is found only on the Pacific coast.

SIZE: Plants less than a foot tall, spreading along the soil, usually wider than high; fleshy stem segments each one-quarter to one-half of an inch long

COLOR: Stems, scalelike leaves, and minuscule, naked flowers pale green; entire plant turning crimson in the fall

SITTING ON THE SHORE of Puget Sound at the edge of the Nisqually Delta and munching on the crisp, tangy stem segments of pickleweed, I chuckle to myself as I remember something that botanist and author Gary Paul Nabhan said to me: "I've never written about a plant I haven't eaten." Gary would like pickleweed, I think.

Pickleweed is ubiquitous on the salty flats of bays and estuaries along the Pacific coast, blanketing whole expanses just below the high-tide line with its dusty-green, succulent stems. Although it is one of the commonest plants of salt marshes, most people never notice it, except in autumn. As the days grow shorter and the sun moves south, pickleweed responds to the lessened daylight in the same way as broadleaf deciduous trees: it stops making chlorophyll. As the green pigment disappears from pickleweed's tissues, the underlying red pigments are revealed, turning the formerly obscure plant glorious crimson.

Plants such as pickleweed that grow in alkaline soils are called halophytes, "salt-lovers." Pickleweed is one of the most salt tolerant of all halophytes, thriving in soils comprised of up to 6 percent salt (most plants die in soils containing just 2 percent salt).

Many saline environments are salty because they are so dry. The little moisture in their soils never has a chance to move downward and flush out the salts, but instead is pulled upward and evaporated into the air, concentrating the salts on the surface of the soil. Salt marshes, however, are saline because they are too wet, constantly flooded by salty water. Still, salt marsh environments share many characteristics with arid environments: fresh (non saline) water is scarce, dehydration is a constant threat, and temperatures fluctuate radically on a regular basis (between high tide and low tide in marshes, between night and day in deserts).

Not surprisingly, pickleweed and other salt marsh plants have adapted to their alkaline environment in many of the same ways that desert plants respond to their arid environment. Like desert plants, they are succulent, storing water in their tissues. Their leaves are tiny, to reduce evaporation, and their stems able to photosynthesize to make up for the reduced food production from miniaturized leaves. Their leaf and stem surfaces are covered with waxy coatings or fine hairs to ameliorate the harsh climate. Most salt marsh halophytes, including pickleweed, have close relatives that grow in the deserts.

Salt marsh halophytes also must adapt to physical damage from wind-driven waves and tides, and solve the problem of being inundated in water too salty to drink. Succulence helps pickleweed cope with physical water damage; water rushes right over its smooth, rounded stems. The "water, water, everywhere, but not a drop to drink" problem is more complex. Not only is the seawater too saline to drink, the salty soil itself can actually suck water out of the plants. In a physical process called osmosis, water moves from an area of lower concentration of solutes to an area of higher concentration. Thus, if water in the soil has a higher concentration of salts (solutes) than the plant's tissues, water will be drawn out of the plant into the soil. Pickleweed and most other halophytes deal with this problem by turning osmosis to their advantage. They accumulate sufficient salts in their root tissues to make their internal water saltier than the water in the soil; water then moves from the soil (the area of lower concentration) into their roots (the area of higher concentration). When a pickleweed plant accumulates too much salt, it moves the mineral through its vascular system to an endmost stem segment that falls off and decays, returning the salt to the soil.

Because few insects live in salt marshes, pickleweed doesn't depend on insects for pollination. Instead, it uses an abundant resource: the wind. Its male and female sex organs, unadorned by petals or other flower structures, protrude from the joints of the stem segments, hanging out to catch the stream of air.

Although people eat pickleweed, the saltiness of its foliage repels most wild herbivores. A few kinds of grasshoppers graze on its succulent herbage. A tiny greenish sea slug a bit shorter than an eyelash grazes on the furry mats of green algae that coat the soil in the plant's shade. One tiny mouse, however, the salt marsh harvest mouse, is totally dependent on pickleweed. Found only in the salt marshes of San Francisco Bay, the Pacific Coast's largest estuary, salt marsh harvest mice spend their entire lives (from a few months to a year) in dense pickleweed thickets. During the day, these brown and white rodents snooze in domed, birdlike nests anchored to the pickleweed; at night, they venture out to forage for seeds. Only in the highest flood tides of winter do these small mammals leave the shelter of their pickleweed thickets. Then, as thousands of salt marsh harvest mice swim for higher ground to avoid drowning, sharp-eyed herons, hawks, owls, and gulls feast on the fleeing hordes. The remainder breed so prolifically that by spring, the population has recovered.

Prolific breeding, however, cannot save these endemic rodents from habitat loss. Eighty-five percent of San Francisco Bay's original seven hundred square miles of tidal wetlands have been destroyed. Now protected by the federal Endangered Species List, conflicts between developers and those charged with protecting salt marsh harvest mice have often favored the mouse, leading to its popular moniker of "Mighty Mouse."

While crunching on tangy pickleweed stems, I ponder the creativity in these life stories. That life succeeds at all in such difficult circumstances amazes me.

GIANT ACORN BARNACLE

Balanus nubilus

At low tide the barnacle-covered rocks seem a mineral landscape
carved and sculptured into millions of little sharply pointed cones.
There is no movement, no sign or suggestion of life.

—Rachel Carson, *The Edge of the Sea*

Range: Alaska south to La Jolla, California, and perhaps northern Baja California

Habitat: Rocks, pilings, other animals' shells, from the low-tide line to water three hundred feet deep

Name: Giant acorn barnacles are the largest of their kind, and are named for a fancied resemblance to an acorn. *Balanus* is "acorn" in Greek; *nubilus*, from the Latin word for "marry," alludes to their sexual state: barnacles are hermaphroditic, both male and female.

Size: Cone-shaped shells to four inches high and four and one-half inches wide, and may weigh one-quarter pound

Color: Plates of shell whitish, mantle and feathery feet deep red or purple

Notes: Giant acorn barnacles are one of the two largest species of barnacles on the Pacific coast, and among the largest in the world.

WHILE EXPLORING THE ROCKS at Stinson Beach on a sunny September day, I saw barnacles come alive. A wave washed over a boulder, briefly submerging its bumpy crust of barnacles. As the water covered them, the plates at the top of each cone-shaped shell opened. Several delicate, feathery appendages pushed out from inside and swished through the water. As the water slid away, the feathery appendages retreated, the doors clicked shut, and the barnacles appeared inanimate once more. I watched, fascinated: the water washed over, the barnacle doors opened and their miniature "feather dusters" appeared; the water slid away, the feather dusters vanished, and the barnacles shut up shop.

Barnacles are ubiquitous on the Pacific coast, attaching

themselves in masses to any available hard substrate that is periodically submerged: rocky shores, breakwaters, pilings, boat hulls, buoys, even the shells of other animals. Anyone who has gone tide-pooling barefoot has clambered gingerly over sharp-edged barnacle "pavement." The shells look like those of tiny mollusks, such as mussels, clams, or abalones. But the creature inside with the feather-duster feet is no mollusk. Barnacles are, in fact, crustaceans. In the words of naturalist Louis Agassiz, these odd creatures are "nothing more than a little shrimp-like animal standing on its head in a limestone house and kicking food into its mouth." Only when barnacles open their shells do they reveal their eccentric lives.

A giant acorn barnacle begins life within the shell of its parent, which, although it possesses both male and female reproductive organs, is not usually both mother and father to its offspring. Barnacles are hermaphroditic and thus can produce their own fertile eggs, but they usually stir the gene pool by cross-fertilizing each other, sticking their long sperm tube between the valves of their neighbors' shells. The fertilized eggs develop and hatch in place in the shell of the parent receiving the sperm. The larvae—tiny, motile, shrimplike creatures—swim off on their own, eating and growing with the other zooplankton for several weeks before choosing a place to light. When they are ready to settle down, giant acorn barnacle larvae explore appropriate locations with their sensitive antennae until they find the perfect spot.

Herein the barnacle's life changes dramatically: it glues its head to the substrate with a cementlike substance secreted by glands near its antennae. Other glands secrete the bases of the calcium carbonate plates that will eventually shelter its body. (It may take a giant acorn barnacle three or more years to accrete its large plates.) As the plates grow, the barnacle molts, losing its shrimp-like shell, its antennae, and its eyes. From then on, it is literally stuck to its rock. As they grow large, giant acorn barnacles' shells host colonies of smaller lives such as bryozoans and boring sponges, which give the barnacle a fuzzy brown, olive-green, or red cast.

Once settled, a barnacle does indeed feed by kicking food into its mouth. Barnacles' six crustacean legs have evolved into *cirri,* finely divided, feathery appendages that are thrust through the open mantle, swept through the water to trap plankton and tiny detrital particles, than drawn back into the shell bearing the food. Barnacles lack gills, and so presumably absorb oxygen through their many-branched feet. (Ironically, although giant acorn barnacles are a common research subject, not much is known about their lives since researchers have focused on their muscle fibers, which are among the largest known in animals.)

In evolving their many-plated shells, barnacles have adapted ingeniously to the central problem of life in the intertidal zone: exposure. Many intertidal lives simply leave when the tide is out. Animals that have chosen to remain fixed in place, such as barnacles, mussels, and others, expend great amounts of energy protecting themselves from desiccation, oxygen deprivation, exposure to predators, and extremes of temperature, as well as from the pounding force of the waves—hence the heavy shells, which seal tightly when closed.

One kind of predatory snail has figured out how to defeat barnacles' heavy armor. Dogwinkles, also called rock whelks, simply crawl up to the closed barnacle and bore a hole through the shell with their filelike radula. The snail then squirts digestive juices through the hole, waits, and slurps up the contents. Pacific Northwest Indians once pried giant acorn barnacles off rocks, then roasted and ate the shrimplike innards.

Giant acorn barnacles often settle on the pilings of docks and piers where it is easy to watch them. As the tide moves up to cover these animals, the valves at the top of their shells open, revealing the rich reds and purples of their mantle. Then out come the feathery cirri themselves, sweeping the water with rhythmic movements. They come and go every few seconds, regular as clockwork. En masse, the cirri of giant acorn barnacles seem to dance through the water, like some kind of undersea ballet.

BROWN PELICAN

Pelecanus occidentalis

Brown
PELICAN

(Pelecanus
occidentalis)

A wonderful bird is the pelican;
His bill will hold more than his belican.
　　　　　　—Dixon Lanier Merritt, *Limericks (1910)*

RANGE: Pacific Coast, from Vancouver Island south to South
America; Atlantic Coast, from southeastern United States to
South America
HABITAT: Coastal waters, bays, beaches, open ocean
NAME: Brown pelicans are brownish-gray, *pelican* may come
from the Greek *pelike,* for a wide-mouthed amphora used
to hold water or wine, a reference to the bird's generous bill
pouch. *Pelecanus* is Latin for "pelican"; *occidentalis,* or
"western," is not entirely correct since these birds also occur
on the Atlantic coast.
SIZE: Adult birds forty-five to fifty inches long, beak to tail tip,
with a seven-foot wingspread, weighing up to ten pounds;
eggs three inches long
COLOR: Brownish-gray but for white head and neck; eggs white
NOTES: Brown pelicans can live as long as thirty years.

IN MY MEMORIES of the southern part of the Pacific coast, a line
of pelicans is always flapping past like an aerial string of beads,
flying just above the waves, right offshore. The big, baggy-billed
birds fly as if on patrol, their long, wide wings flapping and gliding in unison, holding course no matter how stiff the wind or
how severe the weather.

Pelicans are peculiar birds. Their bodies are big and heavy for
avian architecture—our brown pelican, with a wingspan of seven
feet and weighing six to ten pounds, is actually the smallest of the
world's thirty species. Below a pelican's distinctive long bill hangs
a bare, wrinkled pouch of skin like a double chin that has lost its
stuffing. This latter is a specialized tool necessary to the pelican's

livelihood. Like so many coastal residents, including gulls, terns, cormorants, diving ducks, grebes, guillemots, auklets, murrelets, osprey, orca, seals, sea lions, sharks, humans, and fish, pelicans are fishermen. Pelicans have an advantage, however, over the many competing fish-eaters: their throat pouch functions as an expandable, built-in dip net, making fishing simpler.

Brown pelicans are unusual even among their own kind. Unlike most other pelicans, which dive from the water's surface, brown pelicans fish from the air. When a brown pelican spots a fish, it folds its wings and plummets into the water from as high as sixty feet. The big bird hits the water beak-first, making a splash large enough to gratify any child doing a cannonball off a diving board. Fortunately for the pelican, the force of its dive is cushioned somewhat by the bird's bill pouch, which balloons like a parachute, and by special air sacs under its skin that give it buoyancy. The bird pops to the surface again almost immediately, folds its wings, and, if it has caught a fish, tips the front of its beak down like a pitcher to pour off the water, then quickly swallows its meal.

These ungainly looking divers are strictly coastal birds. On the Pacific coast, they nest in noisy and odorous colonies on off-shore islands, from Anacapa in the Channel Islands south. Brown pelican pairs court with crouching and bill-stretching displays in late spring. After mating, the pair locates a nest spot on the ground or a cliff ledge within the colony. She builds the simple nest, varying from a scrape in the ground to a small pile of sticks, with materials he supplies. Both parents incubate the two to four eggs she lays, sometimes holding them atop their wide, webbed feet to keep them from absorbing too much heat from the unshaded ground.

After the eggs hatch, the parents alternate feeding runs and childcare. Young pelicans are fed partially digested fish from their parents' throats. Once the young can fly, about two-and-a-half months after hatching, the family leaves the colony and moves north up the coast to fish, sometimes migrating as far as Vancouver Island. In autumn, brown pelicans migrate south down the coast again for the winter.

In the 1960s and 1970s, we nearly lost these unusual birds to pesticide poisoning. Along with peregrine falcons and bald eagles, brown pelicans proved especially sensitive to DDT and other chlorinated hydrocarbons. These poisons, which spurred Rachel Carson to write *Silent Spring*, not only kill insects and the animals that eat them, but have a more insidious, longer-term effect: they accumulate in animals' fatty tissues and interfere with calcium absorption. Thus, fish that ate poisoned insects ingested the poisons and stored them in their own tissues; other fish ate those fish, taking in a higher level of poisons, and brown pelicans ate those fish, receiving a concentrated dose of the lethal chemicals.

Pretty soon brown pelicans were carrying high enough levels of DDT and other chlorinated hydrocarbons that their calcium uptake was seriously impaired. With insufficient calcium, female pelicans couldn't produce the usual numbers of eggs. Those eggs that were laid had such thin shells that parents inadvertently crushed them during incubation. In the space of two decades, brown pelican populations plummeted as quickly as if they had all folded their wings and plunged straight into the ocean. In 1971, for instance, the 552 pairs of brown pelicans nesting on Anacapa Island produced just one live chick.

DDT and related pesticides were banned for most uses in the United States in 1972. By the mid-1980s, brown pelicans had made a dramatic comeback throughout most of their range. In 1986 and 1987, the brown pelican colony on Anacapa Island fledged more than four thousand young. Unfortunately, threats from pesticides still cloud the future of these flying fisher-birds. DDT and other chlorinated hydrocarbons are still widely applied to crops in Latin America, thus contaminating the food supply where pelicans winter. And in the United States, residential use of other pesticides, some of which can degrade into DDT, is sky-rocketing—per-acre rates by homeowners far surpasss rates of application for agricultural use.

I am always amazed at how easily we forget that the world is connected: when we spray our roses for cutworms or our lawn for white grubs, the pesticides don't just "go away." "There is no away," as a friend's father, a physicist, likes to say. "Away" in this case is down the storm sewer into the estuary, into the mouths of zooplankton, which are eaten by fish, and the fish by pelicans. Thus, what I do in my yard comes back to me when the sky off-shore is empty of brown pelicans flying in lines.

Diatoms

Bacillariophyta

Viewed from the distance of the moon, the astonishing thing about the earth, catching the breath, is that it is alive. . . . Aloft, floating free beneath the moist, gleaming membrane of bright blue sky, is the rising earth, the only exuberant thing in this part of the cosmos.

—Lewis Thomas,
Lives of a Cell: Notes of a Biology Watcher

RANGE: Worldwide, in freshwater as well as saltwater
HABITAT: Open oceans, as well as below the high-tide line, on pilings, rocks, eelgrass, and the shells of marine animals
NAME: *Diatom* comes from the Greek word *diatomos,* or "cut in half," for the two halves of this creature's clear shell, which looks like an intricately shaped glass box. *Bacillariophyta,* "the phylum of rod- or staff-shaped lives" in Latin, is the name for this group of unicellular algae, whose shapes, despite the name, vary widely.
SIZE: Diatoms are microscopic
COLOR: Living tissue yellow-brown to olive, shells crystal clear

DIATOMS FASCINATE ME for the same reason that snowflakes do: it seems as if no two are alike. Diatoms' silica shells come in a dizzying variety of shapes, including five-pointed stars, graceful spirals, diamonds, and double-ended ovals. Each glassy shell is ornamented with intricate decorations: spines, pores, ribs, pits, tubercles, or elaborate etched patterns. Unlike snowflakes, which really are all different, individual diatoms within a species are alike, but each of the thousands of species grows its own characteristic crystalline architecture.

Diatoms are microscopic, unicellular algae that evolved the ability to use silica, a common material in the environment, to construct their two-parted protective cases, or shells. The shells, which fit together like a box with a lid, are miniature works of art. Seen under a microscope, each shell looks like an intricately embellished piece of cut crystal.

Inside the glass-walled case lives a one-celled plant, an alga, capable of manufacturing its own food by photosynthesis, and reproducing by splitting itself into two. Diatoms are tinted olive or yellow-brown by the golden pigment of fucoxanthin (also found in giant bladder kelp and others of the brown alga family), which masks their green, chlorophyllous pigments. Unlike land plants, which capture the red and blue-violet parts of the light spectrum with chlorophyll, ocean plants, receiving their light filtered through the water, harvest a different set of light wavelengths. Fucoxanthin, for instance, takes advantage of the abundant green light wavelengths.

Marine diatoms are either free-living individuals that float suspended in the water column of the open ocean, or colonial beings that live in gelatinous masses attached to eelgrass, rocks, pilings, and animal shells in the tidal zone. Colonial diatoms form scummy brown growths much like multicelled, filamentous algae. But when viewed through a microscope, each crystalline shell floats separately, independent, in the colony's gelatin matrix.

Free-living diatoms are an important part of the plankton, the community of largely microscopic organisms that drift with the ocean currents. (Diatoms can swim, but are so small that they are swept along by powerful currents.) Diatoms form the majority of the phytoplankton, the plant plankton. The zooplankton, or animal plankton, is made up of microscopic crustaceans, mollusks, and other marine invertebrates, as well as the larval stages of many marine animals.

Plankton, the most common life in the ocean, is the basic food of marine ecosystems, nourishing creatures as small as protozoans and as large as blue whales. (Within the plankton, diatoms are the single most important foodstuff of the ocean.) Many creatures eat plankton at one time or another during their lives, sieving the microscopic food out of the water with feathery tentacles, trapping it with mucus-coated skin or on body hairs, or simply gulping in great drinks of seawater soup and digesting the edible bits. Grazers eat only phytoplankton; carnivores dine on zooplankton. Many plankton consumers are picky eaters: sperm whales, for instance, prefer krill, a microscopic shrimplike crustacean that is part of the zooplankton.

Diatoms are among the most abundant organisms in the world. These single-celled algae exist in such multitudes that they may contribute more oxygen to the atmosphere than any other group of living beings. The crystalline shells of marine diatoms accumulate in enormously thick layers on the ocean bottom. At great depths—over eighteen thousand feet below the surface—the minute silica shells form pure layers. (The extreme water pressure at such depths dissolves the calcium carbonate shells of other marine animals, leaving only the glassy diatom cases.) The thick layers of microscopic discarded diatom shells are eventually pressed into a shaley rock called diatomite. Bluffs of whitish or buff-colored diatomite that formed at the bottom of deep sea trenches and have since been uplifted are exposed in various places in the Coast Ranges of California, from San Diego to Monterey. A seven hundred foot-thick deposit of diatomite near Lompoc, California, is mined for diatomaceous earth, an organic pesticide used to kill slugs and other garden consumers.

Phytoplankton includes other kinds of minute algae, such as dinoflagellates, single-celled creatures once thought to be neither animal or plant, but now considered algae. Although dinoflagellates are less common overall than diatoms, these minute algae are more likely to be noticed because, when conditions are favorable, they undergo rapid, local population explosions. Some kinds of dinoflagellates can make their own light by chemical reactions, the way that fireflies glow. They are the source of the subtle glow when waves phosphoresce at night. If you dipped a glassful of the glowing seawater and looked at it with a hand lens, you would see that the phosphorescence actually consists of multitudes of tiny, separate sparks. Another kind of dinoflagellate is responsible for the poisonous "red tide"—named for the color that these tiny algae tint the water—that kills fish and shellfish by the multitudes. Unusually warm surface water and high amounts of pesticide and fertilizer runoff cause population explosions of these dinoflagellates; the poisons in their tiny cells kill the creatures that eat them.

If you ever have the chance to examine diatoms under a microscope, do. Don't be surprised if you find yourself glued to the eyepiece, entranced by the crystalline beauty and intricate detail in the shells of these miniature plants. There is nothing else in the world like them—except snowflakes.

Moon Jellyfish

Aurelia aurita

Moon Jellyfish
(Aurelia aurita)

In quiet bays in Puget Sound and British Columbia the jellyfish
Aurelia aurita . . . *sometimes occurs in such immense numbers that*
it is impossible to dip an oar without striking several of the beauti-
ful, pulsating animals. A boat seems to glide through a sea of jelly-
fish rather than through water.

      —Edward F. Ricketts, et al., *Between Pacific Tides*

RANGE: Found in many of the world's oceans; in the Pacific, from Alaska to southern California

HABITAT: Open water near ocean surface, within several miles of shore and in large inland bays

NAME: Moon jellyfish are the shape and color of the silvery full moon; the transparent, quivering bodies of the medusa or jelly stage of these animals' lives gives rise to the name "jellyfish." *Aurelia,* "golden" in Latin, describes the color of the mature gonads; *aurita,* Latin for "little-eared one," refers to the eight lobes in the jellyfish's bell.

SIZE: Bell of medusa stage up to six inches across and domed, with short, fine, fringelike tentacles; polyp stage one-eighth to one-quarter inch long

COLOR: Medusa stage milky-white or clear; polyp stage whitish

NOTES: Jellyfish belong to the same group of animals as sea anemones, corals, sea pens, and hydroids.

WALK THE BEACH after a fall high tide and you may find gelatinous blobs studding the line of flotsam like soft beads on a giant necklace. These are the storm-tossed remains of one of the ocean's seasonal lives, moon jellyfish. Like the drifts of spring wildflowers on land, they appear in masses in late winter or early spring, and spend the warm months riding the ocean currents. By autumn, their lives are over and they wash ashore, their once elegant bells tattered and torn. But lift the edge of the collapsed bell (use a stick or pencil to avoid being stung by the tentacles), and you may see the tiny, whitish tubelike forms of the next generation clinging like seeds to their parent's dead tissues.

Jellyfish, or jellies, as marine biologists prefer to call them, are odd creatures: 95 percent water and salt, with no heart, no brains, no spine, and no bones. Many are denizens of the open ocean, riding the currents great distances, pulsating downward into the dark waters of the depths to feed. Jellies of sunlit surface waters, like moon jellyfish, are usually transparent, making them almost invisible in the open water, where there is no place to hide. Jellies of the shadowy depths may be brightly colored and patterned. Many jellies are tiny, their bell no bigger than a thimble. Others are huge. The largest, the arctic Chrysoara, or lion's mane, can grow tentacles over a hundred feet long, longer than a full-grown blue whale. Its bell can reach up to six feet in diameter.

Like many marine animals, jellies live Dr. Jekyll and Mr. Hyde lives: a sac-shaped, sedentary polyp stage alternates with the ethereal, free-swimming medusa, or jellyfish stage. (*Medusa*, for the snake-haired character in Greek mythology, refers to the jelly's tangled ring of tentacles and toxic sting.) With a graceful, mobile phase alternating with a fixed, immobile phase, jellies seem almost like the butterflies of the sea as they flutter through the water, pulsing their bells to propel themselves. Unlike butterflies, however, the polyp stage does not retire to a cocoon to metamorphose into the jelly; rather, it clones itself by asexual reproduction—budding, in this case—into many jellies.

Moon jellyfish polyps hatch from eggs produced after a male and female jelly mate. The fertile eggs adhere to their mother's gonads and within a few days hatch into pear-shaped, tubelike creatures with long tentacles at one end. These tiny young ride along under the shelter of the mother's bell until they are ready for life on their own (or until she is beached by an autumn storm). Once freed from the shelter of their parent, the tiny polyps swim about in the shallows in search of a place to attach for the winter.

Once a moon jelly polyp's sensitive tentacles detect a suitable home—a rock or shell on the bottom, the underside of a piece of decaying wood, a wharf or float—the little vase-shaped creature attaches its swimming end and stays put for the remainder of its life (usually only one winter). The polyp waves its hairlike stinging tentacles through the water, angling for small crustaceans and other zooplankton, which it immobilizes and carries to its saclike stomach to digest.

Come spring, the moon jelly polyp goes through a remarkable change: its tubelike body develops transverse constrictions dividing it into a stack of circular, lifesaver-shaped disks. When conditions are right, the disks separate from their parent and swim off on their own. These dozens of free-swimming young, all genetically identical to their parent polyp, grow into the medusa stage.

Each moon jelly medusa spends the spring and summer in coastal waters, eating and growing. Many jellies hunt by immobilizing swimming prey with their nematocysts, stinging cells found in clusters on the skirt of tentacles hanging from the outer margins of a jelly's bell. Moon jellyfish, however, trap copepods and other small crustaceans in the mucus that coats their bell. Microscopic hairs move the food to the underside of the bell and into the jelly's mouth. Moon jellyfish tentacles are short and fine as hairs, and are apparently mainly for defense. Their nematocysts are, however, strong enough to raise stinging welts on human skin. Some jellies pack far more powerful punches. An Australian jelly, the sea wasp, carries such a fearsome neurotoxin that its sting can kill a person in five minutes.

With their stinging defenses, jellies have few enemies. Gulls and other seabirds sometimes dine on rafts of jellies, but jellies' main predators are sea turtles, blue rockfish, molas, and humans. (Dried and salted jellyfish are considered a delicacy in China, Japan, and Korea.) The predator most identified with jellies is the mola, or ocean sunfish, a creature of the open ocean with a queer truncated body that ends abruptly just back of their dorsal and anal fins, as if the latter half of the fish was swallowed by some enormous predator. These fish grow to thirteen feet long and weigh up to 3,300 pounds on a diet of jellies and distantly related comb jellies. Their odd shape may keep them from getting tangled in jellies' tentacles. Molas' skin is covered with mucus to protect the fish from the sting of its meal.

When moon jellyfish populations bloom, their ghostly bodies may crowd the ocean's surface in concentrations as dense as terrestrial hillsides packed with wildflowers. Jelly blooms occur most frequently in quiet inland waters on the northern Pacific coast. Unlike terrestrial wildflowers, however, the life of such jelly blooms is measured in hours, not days or weeks. The changing tides bear the floating animals away as suddenly as they appeared, like visitors from a fascinating and foreign world that we can visit, but never truly know.

HARBOR SEAL

Phoca vitulina

young pacific
HARBOR SEAL

(Phoca vitulina)

In the water, a harbor seal can be identified by the low profile of its gently rounded head, a broad snout, and enormous dark eyes that blink inquisitively at intruders. A seal normally disappears quickly and silently, leaving only a small swirl as it sinks beneath the surface.

—Tony Angell and Kenneth C. Balcomb III,
Marine Birds and Mammals of Puget Sound

RANGE: Across the North American Arctic and down the Pacific Coast to southern California; down the Atlantic to the Carolinas

HABITAT: Bays, inlets, protected coastal waters, river mouths, and in the Arctic; also in freshwater lakes

NAME: Harbor seals are named for their preference for the quiet water of bays and harbors; *seal* comes from an Old English word for a magical ocean creature that can take on a human form. *Phoca* is Greek for "seal"; *vitulina* means "calf-bearing" in Latin.

SIZE: Adults four to six feet long, weighing ninety-nine to two hundred-fifty pounds (males larger than females)

COLOR: Fur silver to iron-gray above and mottled with darker spots, creamy below

VOICE: Usually silent, except for occasional coughing, bleating, or sighing sounds

AS A CHILD, I loved to listen to my Grandmother Chris's Scottish folktales. Among my favorite stories were those about *selchies* (pronounced "silkies"), magical creatures that could assume the form of both sleek seal and enchanting human. Selchies, it seemed, would woo Scottish lads or lasses into marriage, but eventually, pining for its old aquatic life, the selchie would disappear, leaving behind a heartbroken spouse.

Harbor seals could well be the inspiration for my grandmother's selchie stories. They inhabit sheltered coastal waters, near where humans live. Although shy and easily disturbed when hauled out on land, once in the water, these mammals swim right up to boats or divers, apparently indulging their curiosity. The harbor seals' habit of surfacing quietly in a vertical position, as if standing in the water with only their head and large dark eyes showing, then exhaling in a soft sigh or cough and sinking out of sight without a sound, makes them seem eerily human.

Harbor seals are pinnipeds, part of the group of "flipper-footed" marine mammals that includes earless or true seals like harbor seals; walruses; and eared seals, such as sea lions. Scientists believe that these swimming carnivores took to the oceans some twenty million years ago, long after whales and dolphins moved from land to sea. Pinnipeds evolved paddlelike feet for swimming and thick layers of blubber for insulation in the cold ocean waters, but retained some ability to move about on land.

Earless seals and eared seals seem similar, but the two kinds of pinnipeds possess differing physical features and behavior. Eared seals are named for the small flap, or pinna, that projects from above their ears. But they are most easily distinguished from earless seals by their flippers and their gait: eared seals' front flippers are much larger than their back ones and their back flippers rotate forward, allowing them to walk on land with a shuffling gait. In contrast, earless seals sport small and nonrotating flippers, which force these seals to scrunch along on their bellies out of the water like overweight inchworms. Researchers think that earless and eared seals evolved from entirely different ancestors: earless seals from an otterlike creature, eared seals from bearlike animals.

Only two of the nine North American species of earless seals are commonly seen on the Pacific coast south of Alaska: the harbor seal and the elephant seal. The two are as unalike as relatives can be. Elephant seals are huge—bulls weigh up to four tons—loud, and crude. These behemoths spend the majority of their lives at sea, traveling thousands of miles from their breeding grounds to their feeding areas. In winter, elephant seals haul out in densely crowded rookeries to mate. Bulls honk and bellow through the amplifying chambers in their enormous noses, and engage in bloody fights with rival bulls, all for sex. No one watching or listening to an elephant seal could cast one of these creatures as a selchie, a changeling enchantress.

Harbor seals, by contrast, are small, about the length of an adult human, positively sylphlike compared to elephant seals, and quiet. (If you spot a harbor-seal-sized mammal and it is barking, it is a sea lion.) Unlike elephant seals, harbor seals are homebodies, spending their entire lives in the same patch of coastal waters. At breeding time, harbor seals may gather in groups as large as five hundred on rookeries, stretches of shoreline where they can haul out undisturbed, but most often they are found in groups of half a dozen or so.

Female harbor seals come ashore in late winter to deliver a pup (or, rarely, two) conceived the previous year. The pups are precocial, able to swim immediately after birth. They nurse for about four weeks, gaining weight quickly on a diet of milk that contains as much as 40 percent fat. After their pup is weaned and on its own, a female harbor seal is ready to mate again. Unlike their larger cousins, male harbor seals do not expend the energy to maintain harems of potential mates. Instead, males mate with any available female; females may mate with more than one male.

Clumsy on land, harbor seals excel in water. A harbor seal can dive as deep as three hundred feet and remain underwater for more than twenty minutes. These finned mammals speed along like living torpedoes, and turn on an underwater dime, faster than the fish they chase. Before disappearing below the surface, a harbor seal exhales, emptying its lungs (the "sighing" sound often heard by boaters). Once under the surface, the seal's breathing stops, its heart rate slows from about fifty-five beats per minute to fifteen, its eyes dilate to compensate for the reduced light, and its hearing adapts to the muffled acoustics underwater.

Despite deep dives and speedy resurfacing, harbor seals never suffer the "bends," an accumulation of nitrogen bubbles in the blood that can be fatal to human divers. By exhaling before they dive, lowering their heart rate, and storing oxygen in their blood and tissues, harbor seals keep their blood well-oxygenated.

Harbor seal fur and blubber was not much in demand by seal hunters of old. Still, thousands of harbor seals were killed each year for their diet before all pinnipeds were protected by law. In order to maintain their insulating coat of blubber and keep their bodies warm, harbor seals consume large amounts of fish, squid, and small octopuses. Fishermen often blame seals for poor catches. Studies show, however, that harbor seals feed mainly on "trash fish" species. In Puget Sound, for instance, harbor seals' diets include black-belly eelpout, various sculpins, flounder, Pacific herring, hake, tomcod, shiner perch, and cod. Of course, these pinnipeds eat whatever they can catch, including the odd salmon from a hook.

Although familiar, harbor seals continue to enchant us, inspiring modern-day selchie stories. Maine folksinger and song-writer Gordon Bok tells one such story in his song "Peter Kagan and the Wind," about a lonely fisherman who went away one summer and brought home a beautiful wife. When Kagan went out fishing in his dory, his wife would sing him home, her voice reaching twenty miles out to sea. "She was a seal, you know," goes the song, "Everyone knew that, even Kagan. But no one would say."

CHUM SALMON

Oncorhynchus keta

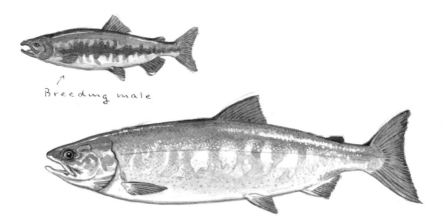

Breeding male

Chum SALMON
(Oncorhynchus keta)

The salmon dwelt in a huge house, similar to those of the Indians, far under the sea. In their home, the salmon went about in human form. When the time came for the annual runs, they put on their salmon skins and converted themselves into fish. . . . The run was thus conceived to be a voluntary sacrifice for the benefit of mankind. . . .

—Philip Drucker,
Cultures of the North Pacific Coast,
quoted in Bruce Brown's *Mountain in the Clouds*

RANGE: Arctic and Pacific oceans from Northwest Territories to Tillamook Bay, Oregon (formerly south to the Sacramento River, California), also northeast Asia

HABITAT: Anadromous; feeds in the ocean, spawns in shallow streams and springs, mostly near the coast, although some populations, including those in the Yukon River, swim far upstream

NAME: *Chum*, from the Chinook word *tzum*, or "spotted," may refer to the vivid purple splotches these fish sport during spawning; *salmon* comes from *salmo*, the Latin name for this family of pink-fleshed, oceangoing fish. *Oncorhynchus*, "swollen-beak" or "hooked beak" in Greek, describes the spawning male's gaping mouth; *keta* is their Russian name.

SIZE: Adults can reach three to three and one-half feet long, and weigh up to twenty-five pounds

COLOR: In the ocean, blue above and silvery below; in freshwater, olive or dusky gray with a black line along the sides; spawning males with burgundy splotches or slashes like claw marks on their sides, a pronounced hump and enlarged canine teeth in a gaping mouth

NOTES: Chum salmon are the second largest of the Pacific Coast's six species of salmon.

SALMON SWAM INTO MY LIFE in the early 1970s when my brother, Bill, fresh out of college, landed a job in fisheries management with the Nisqually Tribe in Washington State. Those were the days of the "fish wars" when the Nisqually and other Pacific Northwest tribes were fighting—often literally, as Indians were arrested, beaten, and threatened with death—for their treaty-guaranteed right to fish for salmon in traditional ways at traditional sites. The tribes eventually won in federal court in 1974, but the war was far from over. Commercial and sports fishermen's groups, already faced with dwindling catches, fought the court's decision. State fisheries officials refused to enforce the findings. It was an ugly time, for salmon as well as for humans.

Why the fight? The salmon were disappearing, their numbers shrinking each year. Pacific salmon, along with timber, were once the Pacific Northwest's most important exports, the basis of its booming economy. Dollars aside, however, salmon touch Northwesterners on a deeper level. "If one animal were chosen to symbolize the Northwest," writes James Luther Davis in *The Seasonal Guide to the Natural Year: Oregon, Washington, British Columbia,* "it would have to be the salmon." Despite their many differences, one thing that the various cultures inhabiting the Pacific Northwest can agree on is the importance of these anadromous fish. Salmon matter to the Pacific Northwest. They are part of the region's soul.

Like white sturgeon, shad, oceangoing trout, and some other fish, Pacific salmon spend part of their lives in freshwater and part in the ocean. Born in clean gravels on the bottom of rivers, lakes, streams, and springs, salmon fry float downstream to the ocean. They spend the majority of their life at sea, dining on plankton and larger prey. If they survive an array of predators ranging from common murres to orcas to fishermen, the mature salmon make their way back to the mouth of the very stream in which they were born, swim upriver, spawn, and die. Fisheries biologists believe that salmon use the earth's magnetic fields to chart their course in the ocean, then "smell" their way to the waters of their birth by sensing each stream's distinctive mineral fragrance. Their epic ocean journey, their fidelity to their natal waters, and their once uncountable numbers are all part of what make the story of Pacific salmon so compelling.

Chum salmon, also called dog salmon for the spawning males' grotesquely enlarged canines, are not the biggest, farthest-swimming, or most spectacular of Pacific salmon. But they are the ones I know best. Chum spawn in the slow water of braided side channels, springs, and sloughs. There, in water so shallow that their dorsal fins often wave in the air, female chums fan the stream bottom with their tails, testing the gravel for the proper size and aeration. When a female chum finds an appropriate gravel patch, she digs a "redd," a shallow depression, with her tail.

Her digging activity attracts one or more males, who circle her as she excavates, jockeying for the best position. A chum male will attempt to dominate the patch of stream where a particular female is excavating her redd. He circles the female, lunges at intruders, and attacks challengers with his fierce canine teeth. His vivid spawning coloration trumpets his success—or his failure—like a billboard. Male chums driven from a redd immediately lose their burgundy badges; only when the male regains his territory does the color reappear. Back at the redd, as the female chum exudes hundreds of orange eggs into the nest, the attendant male squirts clouds of sperm over them.

Buried chum eggs hatch in about two months into alevins, tiny creatures that remain in the gravel, subsisting on the nutrients in their yolk sac. Of the thousands of eggs, 10 percent at most survive to the fingerling stage, where the miniature fish float downstream. Their transition from fresh- to saltwater fish takes place in estuaries, where the rich mingling of land and sea makes for abundant food. Months later, ready for ocean life, chum follow the prevailing North Pacific currents in thousand-or-more-mile-long circles, called "gyres" by biologists, eating and growing for three to five years. The amount of time chum spend in the ocean, following the currents round and round, depends on their growth, which depends on the ocean food supply. Puget Sound chum, for instance, spending their first spring in the food-rich environment of the sound, usually remain in the ocean only three years. Eventually, fat and gleaming, chum salmon are impelled home to the place of their birth.

Once a chum enters freshwater, it battles its way upstream without eating or resting, focused solely on spawning. After seeding the next generation, a spawned-out fish drifts listlessly, thin, battered, its tail and fins worn to the bone. Its life is over. But the nutrients harvested in the ocean live on. As its body rots, the salmon nourishes other lives, from vine maples and salmonberry crowding the streambanks to grizzly bears.

Pacific salmon once spawned in such numbers that their swimming and leaping bodies crowded streams bank to bank. Early American settlers complained that the noise of spawning salmon kept them awake at night. Biologists estimate that each year some fifteen million salmon once thrust their way up the Columbia River alone, heading upstream as far as Idaho. A fish wheel on the Columbia in 1882 took 6,400 salmon from the river in just one day. Predators from grizzly bears to bald eagles to deer mice to humans flocked to streambanks to feed on the bounty. The numbers of salmon, wrote the Smithsonian Institution's Richard Rathbun in 1899, are "so great as to challenge human ingenuity to affect them in any way."

Unfortunately, human ingenuity was up to the task. By the time the protagonists in the fish wars were sitting down over conference tables in the 1980s to divide up the salmon harvest, there was almost nothing left. Rivers that had seen millions or thousands of salmon return each year hosted as few as dozens. A century of habitat destruction had taken its toll: dams blocked access to spawning grounds; logging denuded entire watersheds, pouring tons of silt on spawning gravels; grazing bared streambanks and warmed waters; irrigation withdrawals dried up whole streams; paving and pollution alike fouled watersheds; estuaries were diked and filled. The ocean-warming phenomenon of recent El Niños dealt the final blow, decimating the bounty of marine food. Today, the salmon runs from six Pacific Coast drainages are on the Endangered Species List; twelve more are proposed for listing.

Will the "salmon people" return? No one knows. When I think of Pacific salmon, I remember a chill, foggy morning in the mid-1980s, when my brother took my husband, Richard, my daughter, Molly, and me, and my niece, Sienna, to visit a spring along the Nisqually River. We stepped out of Bill's truck into a thick fog that muffled sight and sound. All was silent but for curious thrashings, gruntings, and splashings nearby. Across the road, in water so shallow that they were barely half-submerged, huge, tattered fish dug and circled and fought and mated: chum salmon, called home from the ocean to the springs where they were born. Overhead, perched like sentinels in the snagged tops of Douglas fir trees, the dark shapes of bald eagles and crows waited to feed. It could have been the beginning of the world, where the salmon people first began.

WINTER

Winter dumps rain, day after day after day of it, all along the Pacific coast; it brings giant waves that claw at the cliffs, storms that saturate hillsides, causing mud and houses to slide into the sea—but it also ushers in days with air so crystal clear that it seems as if you can see right around the curve of the earth. Winter is no more constant than any other season along the Pacific coast, except for the constancy of the ocean continually thrashing at the shore. The very wildness of the season makes winter my favorite time on the coast. It is an ideal time to contemplate the ocean, and to understand—at least as much as we terrestrial beings can—the majestic size and force of this, the largest of the earth's bodies of saltwater.

Winter is a tough time for the wild residents of the Pacific coast, whether on land or at sea. In the north, winter is the harshest season, the time of least clement weather. On land, winter storms may bring ice or even snow to the coast, freezing plants and animals better adapted to more temperate weather. Rains saturate soils, topple trees, and swell rivers to flood stages. Even marine lives are affected by winter, as water temperatures chill, the higher high tides and lower low tides of winter make the tidal zone more extreme, and storm waves surge through the shallows.

Thus, winter is a restless time for many Pacific Coast lives. Some creatures—as large as whales to as small as hummingbirds—move away altogether to escape winter's extremes. Others, such as Harford's greedy isopod or the giant Pacific octopus, hunker down for the winter, spending most of their days tucked in a sheltering nook in the rocks. Those rooted in place, from giant bladder kelp to redwoods, simply weather the adverse times, taking their chances that they won't be ripped up by the waves or felled by storm winds. Many marine plants, including eelgrass, die back for the winter, surviving as rhizomes buried in mud or as holdfasts securely attached to the ocean bottom.

Toward the end of winter, a new kind of restlessness emerges as coastal lives begin to anticipate spring and the return of warmer, less turbulent weather. That usually turns their minds toward, well, reproduction. As the gray whales are beginning their northward journey to feed in Arctic waters, monarch butterflies' impulses turn to mating and flying inland to start a new generation. Sea lions, once endangered by excessive hunting for the fur trade and now abundant again, haul out for bellowing contests on secluded beaches. Jelly polyps bud new jellyfish to ride the spring and summer waves.

Winter on the Pacific Coast is a time when the ocean reminds us of its power. Stand on a sea cliff during a winter storm and watch the waves explode against the rocks below, and wonder that the Spanish explorers named this the *Pacific* Ocean—from the Latin *pacem,* or "peaceful." Walk a wide beach, especially in the intense darkness of a moonless winter night, to hear and feel the relentless thunder of the ocean, the pulsing of the waves. Walk that same beach on the first sunny day after a storm to see the exquisite clarity of storm-cleansed air, and to marvel at the variety of ocean lives—and humans' trash—tossed up on the beach.

In winter it is easiest to see, as John Murray writes in *A Thousand Leagues of Blue,* that we know so little about the Pacific. "All the books ever written on the subject could be placed in one large wooden crate," says Murray, "and dropped into the waves would have just that much effect on the universe. An insignificant splash." In winter, the Pacific is truly an awesome ocean.

Giant Bladder Kelp

Macrocystis pyrifera

Giant Perennial KELP
(Macrocystis spp.)

Descending for the first time into a sea forest can be a disconcerting experience. The silent, swaying fronds of kelp appear ready to reach out and snare an intruder. Then you see fish of every size and color gliding nonchalantly through openings in the foliage, and soon you are doing the same.

—Dennis Brokaw and Wesley Marx,
The Pacific Shore: Meeting Place of Man and Nature

Range: The Pacific Coast, from Alaska south to northern Mexico, most common in southern California

Habitat: Sloping, sandy or silty ocean bottom to one hundred feet deep

Name: Giant bladder kelp refers to this alga's surprising size and to the inflated globe beneath each leaf that keeps the leaf blades afloat. *Macrocystis* means "big bladder" in Greek; *pyrifera*, "pearlike" in Latin, refers to the bladder's shape.

Size: Plants reach two hundred feet in length; the rubbery, hollow stipes are the diameter of thick ropes and freely branching, with straplike leaf blades from top to bottom

Color: Olive-green to reddish-brown

Notes: Giant bladder kelp are the largest of more than twenty thousand alga species worldwide.

ONE OF THE PACIFIC COAST'S best-kept secrets is its kelp beds, the dense underwater "forests" of giant seaweeds that grow offshore in shallow waters from Baja California to Alaska. Rivaling temperate rain forests in height and tropical jungles in diversity and productivity, these shadowy groves are dominated by giant seaweeds whose stems rise a hundred or more feet from the ocean bottom to the water's surface. Like the forests of giant trees that line the central and northern coasts, these undersea groves occur in a band of varying width along the coast. Because they thrive in the alien realm of the ocean—inaccessible by road or car—these majestic forests are less well known than their terrestrial counterparts.

The most spectacular of the kelp jungles occur from central California southward, and are dominated by giant bladder kelp, a colossal alga with stems stretching 150 to 200 feet from its conical holdfast—its underwater roots—to the end of its stipe. Giant bladder kelp's slender, ropelike stem is as leafy as a bamboo, sprouting olive-brown leaves from top to bottom. At the base of each scimitar-shaped leaf blade is a gas-filled bladder that keeps the blades afloat to catch the maximum amount of sunlight for photosynthesis.

Swimming through the shafts of light piercing the dusky canopy of a grove of giant bladder kelp, divers say, is not unlike walking in a redwood forest on land—except that these "trees" sway with the force of passing waves of water, not wind. And unlike slow-growing, long-lived redwoods, giant bladder kelp are the speedsters of the plant world, spurting upward as fast as eighteen inches per day. Nor do they live as long as terrestrial trees: each enormous plant, battered by waves and gnawed by legions of marine grazers, survives an average of just seven years.

From central California northward, the kelp forests are dominated by bull kelp, which grows a leafless, hoselike stipe up to one hundred feet long with a single bladder at its upper end, from which sprouts a topknot of leaf blades that lie on the water's surface. Unlike giant bladder kelp, bull kelp is an annual, achieving its immense length in just one year.

Marine biologists consider giant kelp beds to be the underwater equivalent of tropical jungles in terms of number, density, and variety of lives. These shadowy groves provide nursery, lunch counter, and trysting grounds for more than 750 species of fish and invertebrates. From bright-orange garibaldi to clouds of amorous squid, and from fuzzy coatings of microscopic diatoms to succulent abalone, kelp forests nurture an astonishing variety of marine lives. Sea otters, for instance, cannot survive without kelp beds: they dive for sea urchins and abalone among the tangled stalks, take shelter in the kelp beds when pursued by predators such as orcas, and anchor their newborn young with kelp fronds to keep them from floating off. Nor can kelp forests survive without sea otters: where predators such as sea otters have been eliminated, populations of sea urchins, voracious grazers of giant bladder kelp, have "clearcut" acres and acres of sea bottom once shaded by the kelp forests.

Sadly, giant kelp beds in parts of southern California are as threatened as tropical jungles, dying off from a lethal combination of natural forces and human impact. Warm-water outflows from nuclear power plants and other sources, in combination with the warmer water brought by El Niño episodes, have heated the ocean enough to weaken or kill giant bladder kelp. At the same time, populations of sea urchins have boomed. When the junglelike forests die off, the myriad of lives they shelter vanish as well. Further, without the thick stands of kelp to absorb the force of incoming waves, winter storms are more likely to tear into beaches—and undermine beachfront homes.

Bathed in a constant wash of nutrients carried by the seawater, kelp beds are enormously productive: the average annual yield of kelp tissue has been estimated at four to six *tons* per acre of sea bottom. Scientists estimate that the seaweeds and sea grasses growing along the coasts cover only about 5 percent of the earth's surface but account for over one-third of the ocean's productivity.

Pacific Coast natives once gathered giant kelps for food and musical instruments—a section of bull kelp's hollow stipe with the bladder cut in half, for example, makes a dandy trumpet. Giant bladder kelp beds in central and southern California are still harvested, but by underwater mowing machines that look like huge lawn mowers mounted on barges. The compounds that give kelp its elasticity and tensile strength are used to make fire-resistant textiles and paper, to thicken ice cream and other foods, and to make cosmetics.

Giant bladder kelp and its northern counterpart, bull kelp, share a curious life story, more like ferns than flowering plants.

They are sporophytes, plants that grow two dissimilar generations. The giant kelp produce spores, miniature one-celled plants that are cloned from the parent plant. A spore swims away from its parent plant, settles on a rock on the ocean bottom, and then divides itself, growing into a minute unisexual plant—either male or female—very unlike its giant alter ego. Sperm produced by the microscopic male plants "smell" the eggs on the female plant and swarm toward their chemical perfume. The union of this generation's egg and sperm grows into the colossal alga we know as giant kelp.

In winter, Pacific storms uproot whole kelp plants, piling the long, rubbery stipes in windrows on beaches. There, kelp nurture a different community of lives: detritus feeders, including swarms of kelp flies and beach hoppers. Kelp flies spend their entire lives on piles of decaying algae. Females lay their eggs on the kelp; the tiny maggots, or larvae, eat its sugary tissues; the larvae pupate and metamorphose into adults right on their natal compost pile.

I've never swum through a giant kelp jungle, but walking Pacific coast beaches after winter storms, I've found whole kelp stems washed ashore. Examining these alien seaweed trees, I can imagine their fantastic undersea world, where shafts of sunlight illuminate the bright colors and strange shapes of fish and other marine lives among the gently swaying stalks of tall algae. Hefting the heavy stipe of a giant kelp, I feel connected to that magical realm.

SANDERLING

Calidris alba

Sanderling
(Calidris alba)

Sanderling in breeding plumage

There is symbolic as well as actual beauty in the migration of the birds; in the ebb and flow of the tides, responding to sun and moon as they have done for untold millions of years. . . . There is something infinitely healing in these repeated refrains of nature, the assurance that after night, dawn, and spring after the winter.

—Rachel Carson,
"Words to Live By,"
This Week magazine, May 25, 1952

RANGE: Worldwide in the Arctic and along continental coasts; in
    North America, breeds in the Canadian Arctic, in migration
    found on both Atlantic and Pacific Coasts
HABITAT: Migration, sandy ocean beaches and shores of inland
    lakes; nesting, dry tundra
NAME: *Sanderling* comes from the Icelandic *sanderla* for this
    bird's preference for sandy beaches and dry tundra. *Calidris*
    is Greek for "shorebird"; *alba*, or "white," refers to these
    small sandpipers' ghostly winter coloring.
SIZE: Adults seven to eight and three quarters inches long, with
    a fifteen-inch wingspread, weighing two to three ounces;
    eggs one and one-third inches long
COLOR: In breeding plumage, back is mottled brown and red-
    gold, underparts white; in winter, back plumage is pale gray
    with dark "shoulders"

SANDERLINGS, ALSO CALLED "GRAY GHOSTS" for their pale winter
plumage, crowd the Pacific Coast in dense throngs from midwin-
ter through spring. These small, skittery shorebirds are one of the
most common wintering sandpipers on the coast. (Only western
sandpipers, equal-in-size but browner, are more numerous.) Like
many North American shorebirds, sanderlings live long-distance
lives, spending nine months of the year bumming the beaches of
the Americas, then winging thousands of miles to the Arctic to
breed and nest.

It is impossible to speak of shorebird migrations without
superlatives: some of the smaller members of the group, such as
white-rumped sandpipers, barely the length of my hand, fly

enormous distances, up to fifteen thousand miles annually. American golden-plovers set flight altitude records, winging higher than 25,000 feet while crossing the Andes. The longest nonstop bird migration flight may well belong to Hudsonian godwits, which cruise eight thousand miles without a break while winging between Arctic nesting grounds and South American beaches.

In this group of routinely epic migrators, sanderlings were not considered exceptional until recently. Ornithologist Pete Myers and his colleagues marked sanderlings and found that these small sandpipers circumnavigate the Americas each year, their migration path describing a great clockwise gyre around the continents. After nesting in the far north, sanderlings fly east across the top of North America and down the Atlantic coast to winter on the coasts of Chile and Peru. After the turn of the year, they fly north again up the Pacific coast, headed for their Arctic nesting grounds.

Why fly such a grueling commute each year? By winging north to the Arctic and near-Arctic for the brief northern summer, shorebirds take advantage of the incredible abundance of food produced in the few weeks between snowmelt and the first hard frost—insect populations, in particular, explode then, as anyone who has traveled to the area can attest. The fierce and long winters limit the number of year-round residents, leaving plenty of resources for migrants and their hungry nestlings. Too, ground-dwelling predators, including snakes, lizards, and large rodents, which can decimate populations of ground-nesting birds such as sanderlings, are scarce in the far north.

Time is of the essence, however. Sanderlings and other migrants have two or three months in which to breed, raise nestlings, and vacate the area before winter returns. Hence the mass movement south in late summer. Since more than twenty million shorebirds migrate through the Americas each year, finding food and unoccupied territory for the other nine months of the year is no simple endeavor. Most shorebirds go long distances, stopping only to "fuel up" at locations with bountiful food supplies. Ornithologists say that 80 percent of migrating North American shorebirds stop at about half a dozen such fueling sites on their long commutes, including Alaska's Copper River Delta, Bowerman Basin near Grays Harbor in Washington State, San Francisco Bay, and the Delaware Bay on the Atlantic coast. The food at these estuarine layovers is vital to the survival of literally millions of shorebirds.

Not all sanderlings winter as far south as South America. Some travel a mere couple of thousand miles to our Pacific Coast. These familiar flocks of "gray ghosts" skitter up and down sandy beaches from late fall to late spring, feeding right in the wave splash. Sanderlings often feed alongside other shorebirds, such as longer-legged and taller willets, or long-beaked marbled godwits. Mixed flocks of shorebirds can forage together because they partition the food resource: each species dines on a different kind of food. Their beaks are tailored to their particular diet. The sanderling's short beak is best for picking food off the surface of the sand. They chase the waves to pick up small crustaceans such as Pacific mole crabs, thumbnail-sized crabs that surface as the waves wash over them. Sanderlings also pick up beach fleas and isopods from decaying beach debris.

The willet's medium-length bills are all-purpose tools, giving them just enough leverage to probe for small mollusks under the surface, or to snatch fiddler crabs out of crevices between rocks. The long, straight bills of marbled godwits are digging tools, perfect for drilling into soft sediments to extricate succulent marine worms from their burrows. Oystercatchers sport sturdy pry-bar bills, designed to open bivalve shells. American avocets sieve plankton-sized particles out of silt or mud with delicate, long, upcurved bills.

When I spot shorebirds feeding on a winter beach, I always search for the pale, ghostly gray ones running on tiny black legs right in the foamy edges of the waves—sanderlings. As I watch the fluttering of their small, pointed wings, I imagine their annual journeys around the margins of the Americas, from the Arctic down the Atlantic coast as far as South America, then up the long Pacific margin back to the Arctic again. Their annual flights chart the rhythms of life on this blue planet, as surely as the paths of the stars across the night sky.

SPANISH SHAWL

Flabellinopsis iodinea

Elegant Eolid or "Spanish Shawl"
(Flabellinopsis iodinea)

Orange and speckled and fluted nudibranchs slide gracefully over the rocks, their skirts waving like the dresses of Spanish dancers.
—John Steinbeck, *Cannery Row*

RANGE: British Columbia to Baja California

HABITAT: Pilings and rocks, from the low-tide line to kelp beds 110 feet deep

NAME: Spanish shawls are named for the brilliantly colored fringe of cerata, fingerlike projections of their digestive system, that protrude from their back. *Flabellinopsis,* or "fanlike," also refers to the fringe of cerata; *iodinea,* or "iodine-like," to their brilliant purple and red coloration, which makes them look as if they were stained by iodine.

SIZE: Adults to two inches long and half an inch wide, sluglike except for their fringe

COLOR: Body vivid purple, cerata orange, first pair of antennae violet, second pair deep red and coiled

NOTES: Spanish shawls are nudibranchs, or sea slugs, relatives of snails lacking external shells.

PEER INTO THE CRYSTALLINE WORLD of a tide pool at low tide and, if you watch for long enough, you may see a brilliantly colored, sluglike creature ripple across the rocks underwater. These creatures come in vivid hues: some are fluorescent orange with bubbly warts on their back, others rose-red with fingerlike projections, still others white with red plumes, dark blue with yellow streaks, or purple with orange fringes. These gaudily pigmented and oddly decorated creatures are sea slugs, or nudibranchs, cousins of terrestrial slugs and among the most beautiful—and oddest—lives in the sea.

Despite their eye-catching colors, nudibranchs are often overlooked because of their small size—most stretch no longer than the last joint of your little finger. (Spanish shawls are large for their kind, reaching two or rarely three inches long.) Once noticed, however, nudibranchs are not easily forgotten: their brilliant colors, unusual anatomy, and eccentric habits make them memorable.

The dozens of species of nudibranchs come in three types, determined by the shape of their breathing apparatus, which in all cases is external, allowing them to absorb oxygen from the water flowing by (*nudibranch* means "naked gills"). The most common type has a fringe of tentacle-like gills surrounding their anus. Usually yellow with somewhat pimply skin, these flattened nudibranchs are called sea lemons, and do indeed look something like fleshy, squashed lemons. Another type, eolids, like the Spanish shawl, wear their breathing apparatus across their back, protruding like fleshy shawl fringes. These projections, called cerata, are actually dual-purpose, serving as both gills and as extensions of the animal's digestive system. A third kind of nudibranch also sports external digestive system/gill structures on its back, but in these creatures, the limbs branch in many-armed, treelike structures, unlike the simple fingerlike cerata of eolids.

Most marine creatures are colored for camouflage, from jellies so transparent that they disappear against the featureless background of the open sea to octopuses able to change color in seconds. How can nudibranchs, small but succulent, survive when their coloring shouts their presence? The vivid colors of some nudibranchs are actually camouflage, matching their food: an eye-poppingly orange sea slug, for instance, spends its life grazing on orange colonial sponges and is thus camouflaged as it crawls across its dinner. In others, the bright coloration is a warning that they are poisonous. Spanish shawls and some other eolids, for example, have evolved the elegant trick of turning their food into defensive weapons. These nudibranchs feed on hydroids and sea anemones, especially the tips of the larger animal's tentacles, which end in nematocysts, stinging cells. After nibbling a meal of tentacle tips, the eolid digests the edible tissues, but the nematocysts are carried whole and still usable to the tips of the nudibranch's cerata, its digestive system extensions, waving like tentacles above its back. There, the "borrowed" nematocysts lodge, ready to explode and sting any creature that brushes against them. The nudibranch thus equips itself with formidable defensive weaponry as it dines!

Even nudibranch sex is unusual. Spanish shawls and other nudibranchs, like most of their gastropod relatives, are hermaphroditic, each individual equipped with both male and female sex organs. Nudibranchs in the mood, however, do not mate with themselves. Instead, they seek another like-minded nudibranch, and the pair couples end to end. Hermaphrodism probably evolved where potential partners were scarce, enabling a single individual to reproduce sexually, thus allowing some mixing of genes in its offspring. But without a partner, no new genes are introduced, resulting in a high probability of birth defects and other flaws related to genetic inbreeding. Hermaphrodites mating with a partner have many advantages over single-sex individuals: the chance of finding a partner is doubled, since each individual can mate with any other individual of the same species, regardless of their sex. Further, since mating nudibranchs each produce eggs, the result is twice as many offspring.

Nudibranchs are related to sea hares, gastropods that on first glance look like larger, more drably colored sea slugs. Unlike nudibranchs, however, sea hares are herbivores, grazing on the tissues of marine algae. Nor are sea hares tiny, like their vividly colored cousins. In fact, a Pacific Coast species, the black sea hare, may take the world's record for gastropod size. Specimens measuring thirty inches long and weighing as much as thirty-three pounds have been caught off southern California. Like some nudibranchs, sea hares obtain their defenses from their food. When threatened, sea hares squirt dense purple ink from a siphon on their back. The ink is derived from phycoerythrin, a pigment in the red algae sea hares graze on.

Next time you peer into a tide pool, look carefully for flashes of bright color. If you are lucky, you'll see the vivid purple form of a Spanish shawl, waving its orange cerata as it slithers along the bottom or swims in its curious undulating fashion through the water. These small creatures reveal a whole new dimension of coastal life.

ISLAND FOX

Urocyon littoralis

Island Fox
(Urocyon littoralis)

Another element contributing to the Golden State's wealth of species is its relative isolation. In many ways California is an island, sequestered from the rest of the world by the Pacific Ocean on the west and a forbidding wall of granite bordered by desert on the east.
—Dwight Holing,
The Smithsonian Guides to Natural America:
The Far West

RANGE: The six largest of the Channel Islands off the coast of southern California

HABITAT: Found everywhere on the islands, from seashore to grasslands and woodlands

NAME: Island foxes are endemic to California's Channel Islands; *fox* comes from the Old High German name for these bushy-tailed, carnivorous canids. *Urocyon* is "tailed dog" in Greek; *littoralis*, "of the seashore" in Latin, most likely refers to their island home.

SIZE: Adult foxes the size of a small cat, stretching about two feet from nose to tail and weighing just four pounds

COLOR: Salt-and-pepper gray fur with reddish markings on head, feet, and tail

NOTES: Island foxes are the smallest of North America's fox species.

EVEN BEFORE CHARLES DARWIN'S famous trip to the Galápagos in the 1850s, islands fascinated scientists. Their isolation makes islands worlds of their own, self contained outdoor laboratories where plant and animal distribution, behavior, and evolution can be studied in a microcosm. On islands, scientists can see which species are mobile enough to reach the island, study how they colonize the new territory and whether their niche on the island is different than on the mainland, and see how speciation works, whether over the millennia, island residents differentiate significantly from their mainland relatives.

Except in the highly glaciated fjordlike valleys of the northern coast, the Pacific Coast boasts very few islands. Along the two thousand or so miles of coastline between Puget Sound and northern Baja California, the only islands are the minuscule Farallons, northwest of San Francisco, and the loose group of the Channel Islands, off southern California. Only the latter are large enough and isolated enough to have developed distinct species and subspecies. But this they have done in abundance: the Channel Islands are home to from eighty to one hundred unique forms of plants, and over a dozen endemic animals, including the diminutive island fox.

Island foxes are an excellent example of the adaptations animals and plants make to survive on isolated environments like islands. At their full size of four pounds and two feet long, these dainty canids are one-third smaller than gray foxes, their closest mainland kin. They most likely evolved their smaller size as an adaptation to the more restricted food resources of their island environment. (Other Channel Islands animal species, including an extinct pygmy mammoth once hunted by ancestors of the Chumash Indians, are also smaller than their mainland counterparts. But some bird species, including the island scrub jay, are larger.) Island foxes' behavior has changed along with their physical makeup: lacking larger predators to harass or compete with them (except for feral cats), island foxes hunt during the day, instead of at night, as other foxes do.

Island foxes retain many similarities to their mainland kin, however. Like most foxes, island foxes are omnivores—eating almost anything, from berries and nuts to crickets, rodents, and gull chicks. Also like most foxes, they are opportunistic, using all of the habitats available on their island territories, from ocean shore to scrubland to abandoned buildings.

Island foxes inhabit the six largest Channel Islands: San Miguel, Santa Rosa, and Santa Cruz, off Santa Barbara; San Nicolas, one of the most isolated of the islands, some seventy-five miles off Los Angeles; and Santa Catalina and San Clemente, closer to shore, between Los Angeles and San Diego. How the foxes reached the islands is a question that continues to intrigue biologists. The probable answer involves the San Andreas Fault, catastrophic changes in sea level, the Chumash and Gabrieleño Indians, and ten or fifteen million years.

The simplest possibility is that island foxes' ancestors swam out to the islands at a time when sea levels were much lower. Some eighteen thousand years ago, during the Glacial Age, when geologists believe that sea levels were as low as they have been in the history of the islands, the four northern islands—San Miguel, Santa Rosa, Santa Cruz, and Anacapa—formed one large island only about five miles off the then coastline. The ancestral foxes might well have been able to swim or float that gap. (Smaller animals have gone further. In 1955, for instance, a live black-tailed jackrabbit, a mainland species, was found alive and afloat on a kelp mat thirty-nine miles off the coast.)

Unfortunately for this theory, fox fossils found on the islands and dated to sixteen thousand years ago are as small as present-day island foxes. Two thousand years is simply not enough time for small foxes to evolve. Further, the island fox bears much more resemblance to a species of small foxes found in southern Mexico and Central America than to mainland gray foxes. Thus, biologists speculate that island foxes may indeed have swum across a narrow channel from the mainland, but between the mainland of southern Mexico and the islands. The geology of the Channel Islands supports this theory. Their rocks show that they, along with the rest of southern California west of the San Andreas Fault, were once attached to mainland Mexico. Movement along that and other fault systems has pushed the Channel Islands hundreds of miles northwestward to their current location in the past ten to fifteen million years. Ancestors of island foxes may have hitched a ride on the landmass that eventually became the islands and were subsequently stranded. Biologists also speculate that island foxes reached the more remote islands by being transported by the resident Chumash and Gabrieleños or their ancestors, who may have kept the diminutive foxes as pets.

Over the millennia, island foxes and a host of other endemic Channel Island species, including the ten-foot-tall giant coreopsis, a yellow-flowered shrub related to daisies, and the tiny island night lizard, have evolved with their adopted habitat. In the last two centuries, however, hundreds of nonnative species, from South African ice plants to American bison, have been introduced to the islands, with disastrous results. Goats, for example, brought to San Clemente in 1827, have practically denuded the island, eliminating forty-eight native plant species. The National Park Service, which manages most of the five northernmost islands; the Nature Conservancy, which manages the majority of Santa Cruz; and the U.S. Navy, which manages San Clemente, are working to restore native plant and animal species to the islands.

I think that any creature or plant that can hitch a ride on an island and survive on that small ark over millions of years deserves our respect, admiration—and protection.

MONARCH BUTTERFLY

Danaus plexippus

Monarch Butterfly
(Danaus plexippus)

Inasmuch as the Monarch Butterflies are a distinct asset to the City of Pacific Grove, and cause innumerable people to visit said city to see the said Butterflies, it is the duty of the citizens of said city to protect the Butterflies in every way possible from serious harm and possible extinction by brutal and heartless people.

—Ordinance 352,
City Council of Pacific Grove, California,
November 16, 1938

RANGE: Nearly all of the Americas, from Hudson's Bay south through South America, except Alaska and the northern Pacific Northwest

HABITAT: Found from ocean coast to mountaintops in migration; when breeding, wherever milkweed plants grow, from scrub deserts to grasslands, also pastures and roadsides

NAME: Monarch butterflies may have been named for England's King George III, who favored orange cloaks with black trim. *Danaus* honors the Greek goddess Diana; *plexippus,* from "network" in Latin, probably refers to the netlike black venation of their orange wings.

SIZE: Butterfly phase three and one-half to four inches across, wingtip to wingtip; caterpillar phase two inches long; chrysalis seven-eighths of an inch

COLOR: Butterflies bright rust-orange above with black venation, wing edgings black with white dots; caterpillar banded with black, yellow, and white; chrysalis jade-green

NOTES: Monarchs are the only butterflies known to make annual round-trip migrations.

MONARCHS ARE PROBABLY AMERICA'S best-known butterflies, both because they are so widespread and because of their amazing north-south annual migrations. Unlike the lives of most insects, the details of monarchs' lives are familiar: hatched from tiny, fluted eggs laid singly on their favored food plants, monarch butterflies spend their youth as boldly striped caterpillars. These crawling creatures' task is to eat and store enough energy to metamorphose into airborne butterflies.

A monarch caterpillar dines exclusively on milkweeds (or closely related dogbane). The milky-sapped plants nourish the caterpillar and also supply foul-tasting toxic compounds that protect the insect from hungry birds and other predators. (The plant manufactures its poisons to deter grazers; monarch caterpillars not only have evolved immunity, but "borrow" the toxins for their own use.) One bite, and a bird quickly spits out a monarch. Other butterflies with similar coloring to monarchs, including viceroys and queens, also eat foul-tasting plants for protection, thus reinforcing the lesson that orange and black butterflies are inedible.

After a monarch caterpillar has munched and grown its way through five molts, shedding its too-tight skin each time, it hangs itself upside down under a plant leaf, and undergoes a magical transformation. First it struggles out of its striped caterpillar skin for the last time, transforming itself into a glistening, jade-green pupa. Inside the hard case, the creature's body essentially melts. A week or so later, the pupa splits and out crawls an entirely different creature, with a slender black body, twin antennae, and fragile wings. The butterfly stretches its wings to full size, beats them a time or two, and the monarch is off, airborne.

The butterfly form of a monarch has one task in life: reproduction. After these winged creatures mate, the female lays her eggs singly on milkweed or dogbane. Neither she nor her mate will live much longer, but no matter. Within days, the eggs hatch into voracious striped caterpillars, and the cycle begins all over again.

The metamorphosis from egg to skin-shedding, crawling caterpillar to glistening pupa to graceful, winged butterfly is just ordinary butterfly magic. To that, monarchs add an astonishing migration. In late summer, the butterflies of the year's last brood undertake an epic trek: monarchs from as far north as northern Canada wing their way south, either to the Pacific coast or to the mountains of Michoacan, in central Mexico. On a journey that is entirely new to them, these insects no sturdier than origami paper fly thirty miles a day, winging thousands of miles and as high as ten thousand feet as they pass over mountain ranges, aiming for wintering areas in fog-watered forests where freezes are rare.

Come spring, their mating instincts and migratory urges wake simultaneously. The monarchs head back north (or inland) to recolonize their summer territory. The overwintering adults don't make the entire trek, but their children and their children's children do. Adults mate near the overwintering sites, and pregnant females fly on, laying eggs as soon as they reach places where milkweeds and dogbane grow. (Males die soon after mating; females after laying their eggs.) Succeeding generations go through the whole magical egg-to-butterfly process, mate, and fly off, taking the species' journey onward until they reach the edge of the monarchs' range.

The monarchs that winter on the Pacific coast from Mendocino, California, south to northern Baja are as much a part of California folklore as the swallows of San Juan Capistrano, says author and entomologist Robert Michael Pyle in *Handbook for Butterfly Watchers,* celebrated in everything "from granite statues and children's parades to Beach Boys' songs." Arriving in October, and staying until about March, these coastal winterers seek out dense groves of trees, usually Monterey pines, Monterey cypresses, or nonnative eucalyptus, in the fog belt along the coast. The more well-known and long-established wintering sites, including the one at Pacific Grove, the town that calls itself "Butterfly City U.S.A.," are tourist attractions.

For all we know about these amazing butterflies, however, mysteries remain. We still do not understand how they navigate those thousands of miles, although recent research shows that monarchs navigate at least partly by the sun's daily movements. They must depend on some genetic coding as well, or how could each year's brood head so unerringly to wintering grounds the individual insects have never seen? Nor do we understand which monarchs winter on the Pacific coast, and why.

When the city council of Pacific Grove passed the ordinance to protect the monarchs in 1938, the migrating butterflies winged across Monterey Bay some two million strong, forming a fluttering orange-brown carpet above the waters. These days, perhaps twenty thousand monarchs winter in what remains of Pacific Grove's once extensive woodlands—ironically, development for the area's tourist industry destroyed much of their wintering habitat—and numbers have declined seriously along the entire coast. In the winter of 1997, for instance, says biologist Mia Monroe, the whole coast hosted between 1 and 1.5 million butterflies, an "incredible" year, but still less than the numbers that once showed up just at Pacific Grove. The monarchs' decline is a familiar story: logging and development have eaten away at the woodlands where the butterflies winter, while pesticides and herbicides take their toll on the caterpillars and their food plants. In 1987, the International Union for Conservation of Nature listed the North American monarch migration as a "threatened phenomenon."

One December weekend, I traveled to Pacific Grove to see the wintering monarchs at their most famous sanctuary. That year, the grove hosted just ten thousand butterflies, a fraction of their former numbers. Two twisted Monterey pines were cloaked with orange and black insects "shingled over each other like dead leaves," as Alison Deming writes in her lyrical poem sequence, *The Monarchs*. I can only begin to imagine what two million monarchs would look like.

GRAY WHALE

Eschrichtius robustus

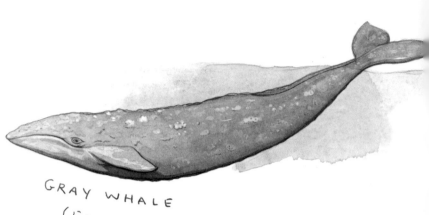

GRAY WHALE
(Eschrichtius robustus)

In 1977, a single gray whale in San Ignacio Lagoon, near Scammon's Lagoon, off Baja California, became "chronically friendly," . . . and allowed itself to be petted by passengers of all the whale-watching boats that could find it. During the next several seasons, the number of friendly whales soared, until anyone who wanted to pet a whale could do so. . . . Now it seems to have become part of their whale culture, something they've learned from each other.
—Diane Ackerman, *The Moon by Whale Light*

Range: Formerly in the Atlantic Ocean and the eastern and western Pacific; now only from the Beaufort and Chukchi seas south to southern Baja California

Habitat: Coastal waters; mates and calves in shallow lagoons

Name: Gray whales are named for their color; *whale* comes from *hvalr*, the Old Norse word for these mammals. *Eschrichtius* is obscure; *robustus* means "strong" in Latin.

Size: Adults thirty-five to fifty feet long, weighing twenty to forty tons (females larger than males); calves average fifteen feet at birth and fifteen hundred pounds

Color: Gray with whitish blotches, also splotched by patches of barnacles and whale lice

Voice: Gray whales communicate in long, low tones (less than 1,000 Hz) that may sound to human ears like groans, bubbles, and knocks.

THAT MAMMALS THE SIZE OF WHALES EXIST at all is extraordinary. These massive creatures, with bodies as long as baseball infields and weighing more than the largest dinosaurs, could only exist in water: on land, their skeletons eventually would collapse under the weight of their tissues and organs. Or they would cook to death. A whale's metabolism generates so much heat that its tissues begin to stew once out of the natural icebox of the ocean.

Gray whales are not the largest whales: that honor goes to the blue whale, the largest animal known to man, stretching as long as one hundred feet and weighing up to one hundred fifty tons. Gray whales are puny by comparison, but only by comparison. A full-grown gray whale weighs about as much as a loaded tractor-trailer rig, and is nearly the length of a school bus. Its tail flukes reach twelve feet from tip to tip and weigh three hundred to four hundred pounds; a careless flick of its five-foot-long flippers can easily drown a swimming human. A gray whale's eye is as large as a grown man's fist; its massive mouth can swallow literally tons of water in one gulp.

Whales, along with dolphins and porpoises, are cetaceans, members of a group of marine mammals whose terrestrial ancestors bucked the general trend of sea-to-land evolution some thirty million years ago and returned to the ocean. Whales come in two types: toothed whales, carnivorous predators such as orca or sperm whales, like Moby Dick, and baleen whales, which use their comblike baleen plates to strain tiny animals out of the soup of the ocean. In a bizarre twist of logic, most of the largest whale species—blue whales, finbacks, right whales, and bowheads—are baleen whales. These enormous beings subsist on the tiniest of prey: plankton, minute crustaceans, and schools of small fish.

A feeding baleen whale is awesome. It opens its jaws wide and sucks in an Olympic-swimming-pool-sized mouthful of water, closes its screen of baleen plates, then expels the water and swallows the creatures trapped by the baleen. It is like fishing with a huge but very fine sieve. Unlike other baleen whales, gray whales are bottom-feeders, dining on amphipods, tiny crustaceans that live in the soft sediments of shallow ocean bottoms. A gray whale dives to the seafloor, rolls on its side, and sucks up the mud like a huge vacuum cleaner. Then the whale rights itself, squeezes out a cloud of muddy water using its tongue, and swallows what remains.

An ocean bottom where gray whales have been feeding looks like it has been attacked by a dredge shovel. These mysterious "bites" in the seafloor puzzled scientists until one recent summer when several gray whales in Puget Sound did their vacuum cleaner imitations next to the shore in water just twelve feet deep at high tide. When the tide receded, the exposed sound bottom was dotted with pits ten feet across and six inches deep, with mounds of displaced sand nearby. Biologists studying the feeding pits estimated that each mouthful of sand netted the whale about eleven pounds of tiny crustaceans called ghost shrimp.

Gray whales spend six or seven months of each year in the north Pacific, as far north as the Chukchi and Bering seas, off the coasts of Alaska and Siberia. In these rich arctic waters, the whales feed almost constantly, sucking amphipods out of the bottom mud and occasionally swallowing schooling fish or small swimming crustaceans. Over the arctic summer, the whales ingest an average of sixty-seven *tons* of their tiny food, putting on six to twelve inches of blubber, stores of oily fat that nourish them for the other half of the year.

In early October, as the pack ice thickens and the days grow shorter, gray whales, like many other Pacific Coast residents, migrate south. Far south. Over the next four months, these mammals swim six thousand miles to the warm water and shallow lagoons on the west coast of Baja California. Pregnant females leave first, headed south in twos and threes, traveling as much as twenty hours and one hundred miles per day, rarely resting and eating. Males and nonpregnant females follow, in groups of up to twelve, sometimes courting with much splashing and thrashing along the way. (Since gray whale gestation takes about twelve months, sexually mature females—those older than six to eight years—breed about every other year.) Juvenile whales, like human adolescents, follow but do their own thing, often going more slowly than the other whales or taking extended feeding breaks in places like Puget Sound or around the Channel Islands.

By early January, the expectant gray whales have arrived in the four main Baja California wintering lagoons. Some have given birth along the way and trail three-quarter-ton calves, but most give birth in or near the coastal lagoons. The baby whales, nourished by drinking fifty gallons of fat-rich milk a day, gain as much as seventy pounds of weight each day, reaching two to three tons and eighteen to nineteen feet by the end of March. Calves and mothers remain in the shelter of the lagoons until as late as May before making the arduous return trek to the Arctic.

Some biologists believe that the gray whales' six-thousand-mile swim from the Arctic to Baja California is in the nature of a commute between feeding grounds and resting grounds. These amazing cetaceans may essentially feed in summer and sleep in winter.

The gray whale's survival is even more extraordinary than their long-distance annual migration. Once abundant in the Atlantic as well as both sides of the Pacific, gray whales migrate closer to coastlines than any other whales and thus have proved relatively easy prey for whaling humans for centuries. In the nineteenth century, whaling escalated as the demand for whale oil and whalebone (baleen, most often used for corsets and stays for women's clothing) reached its peak. By mid-century, whalers had discovered grays' wintering grounds off Baja, and in 1857, Captain Charles M. Scammon learned of Laguna Ojo de Liebre, later called Scammon's Lagoon, where thousands of gray whales came to calve and mate. He and other whalers descended on the shallow lagoon, killing so many female whales and their calves, according to contemporary accounts, that the water ran red with whale blood. By the time gray whales were fully protected in 1946, only a few thousand remained along the Pacific coast of North America. Gray whales were among the first species listed on the Endangered Species List.

Now they are among the Endangered Species Act's success stories. With protection, gray whale populations recovered until in 1993, with an estimated 21,000 gray whales along the Pacific coast, they were removed from the list. Better still, they appear to have forgiven us. At Laguna San Ignacio, one of the wintering lagoons on the coast of Baja California, gray whales now rush up to boatloads of whale-watchers, eager to be petted by the very same species that once hunted them to near extinction. That seems awfully like a miracle to me.

WESTERN GULL

Larus occidentalis

western
Gull
(Larus occidentalis)

Some people consider them the rats of the ocean, leaving unwelcome calling cards on docks and boat decks. To others, they are as romantic as Jonathan Livingston Seagull from Richard Bach's book, swooping and soaring and performing aerobatics as though they feel they must show off before accepting a handout.

—Judy Wade,
Seasonal Guide to the Natural Year:
Southern California and Baja California

RANGE: British Columbia to southern Baja California, Mexico

HABITAT: Open ocean, estuaries, shorelines, rarely seen more than a few miles inland; nests in colonies on offshore islands and protected cliffs on the mainland

NAME: Western gulls live on the extreme western edge of the North American continent; *gull* is from *gwylan*, the Welsh name for these birds. *Larus* comes from the Latin word for "seabird"; *occidentalis* means "western" in Latin.

SIZE: Adults to twenty-seven inches long, with a fifty-four-inch wingspread, weighing two and one-half pounds; eggs almost three inches long

COLOR: Adults, white with a dark "mantle" on their upper wings and pink feet; juveniles streaky brown; eggs buff to olive or gray, with brown splotches

NOTES: A western gull banded as a chick lived nearly twenty-eight years.

GULLS ENJOY a contradictory reputation among their human neighbors. We decry their messy habits and noisy, aggressive natures, but we love their fearlessness and acrobatic flight. No matter what you think of them, however, gulls are as ubiquitous and as characteristic of the edge of the sea as any creature. If I were blindfolded and dropped off somewhere along the Pacific coast, I'd know that the ocean was near by the sound of the gulls crying and the smell of the sea.

Of the eleven species of gulls regularly seen along the Pacific coast, western gulls are the only species unique to the stretch of coast between British Columbia and Baja California. With two-foot-long bodies and wingspreads over four feet wide, western gulls are large, the size of herring gulls or glaucous-winged gulls. Indeed, western gulls are closely related to both. Westerns, in fact, hybridize with glaucous-winged gulls in Washington and British Columbia where the two gulls' ranges overlap. These three gulls are part of a complex of closely related and difficult to distinguish gull species—all large and white with gray wings as adults—that range from Siberia to Iceland, and south to Baja California.

This complex of species, called a "super-species" by ornithologists, includes birds that are distinct in the core of their range, but that, like western and glaucous-winged gulls, may interbreed with other species where the two ranges meet. Since one of the acid tests of determining species has been whether two kinds of birds interbreed or not, are these nine kinds of gulls not really separate species? Well. . . no, say ornithologists, but it isn't clear. DNA research, the newest tool in determining species' definitions, may shed some light on the matter. For now, say Paul Ehrlich, David Dobkin, and Darryl Wheye in *The Birder's Handbook*, "When you are in the field trying to sort out which of these gulls you have in your binoculars, take heart. The gulls themselves also have problems telling who is who."

Western gulls are very much coastal birds. Born in a nest on an offshore island or sea cliff along the coast, a western gull chick begins life with its eyes open, covered with down and able to walk. It spends the first few weeks of its life in and around the nest with two or so siblings, hiding in nearby vegetation (if any is available) while its parents are off scavenging for food. Western gulls usually nest in large colonies—the largest, with some 35,000 birds, is on the Farallon Islands off San Francisco. Nesting colonies are located near ready food sources, such as the nesting colonies of other seabirds, with their edible eggs and chicks, or sea lion colonies, where the gulls dine on afterbirth and meat from dead pups. Because they nest further south than most gulls—all the way to Bahia Magdalena, Baja California—western gull embryos and chicks are more heat tolerant than those of other species. The embryos, for instance, can survive temperatures as hot as 114 degrees.

When a parent approaches the nest, the ever-hungry chicks flock around and beg for food by pecking at a colored spot (red, in the case of western gulls) on the parent bird's bill. This pecking stimulates the parent to regurgitate partially digested food into the chick's mouth. So strong is this "target pecking" behavior, wrote ethologist Niko Tinbergen in his classic study of animal behavior, *The Herring Gull's World,* that gull chicks will peck at a stick with an appropriately colored spot, even though the stick bears no likeness to the parent at all.

Six or seven weeks after hatching, a western gull chick fledges, acquiring the indistinct brown plumage that it will wear for its four years as an immature gull. It stays with its parents until it is around ten weeks old, and then flies off for a life of its own. The young gull will spend its next three or so years bumming up the coast as far north as British Columbia or as far south as the tip of Baja California, scavenging for food in habitats as diverse as garbage dumps and clam beds at low tide, and never venturing more than a few miles inland. After molting into gray and white adult plumage, the western gull finds a mate, picks a nesting site in a crowded colony, scrapes out a depression in the ground for a nest, and starts a family of its own.

When I watch a cloud of gulls noisily scavenging for food and chasing each other to steal choice tidbits, I wonder if our ambivalence about gulls reflects our own nature. Gulls—noisy, aggressive, and opportunistic—display qualities that we humans profess to dislike, yet often reward. Look, for instance, at many professional athletes, who, no matter how violent or aggressive or objectionable their behavior, draw huge salaries as long as they succeed in their game. When we are willing to sort out our tangled relationship with our own nature, perhaps we will also see gulls more clearly.

BANANA SLUG

Ariolimax columbianus

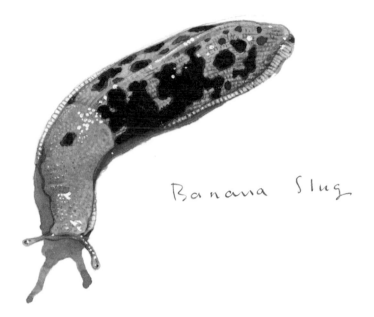

Banana Slug

When we try to pick out anything by itself, we find it hitched to everything in the universe.

—John Muir, quoted in *The Banana Slug*

RANGE: Alaska to central California, with isolated populations
in the coastal mountains of southern California
HABITAT: Moist forests, from the coast inland to the Cascades
and the Sierra Nevada
NAME: Banana slugs are named for their yellowish color and
distinctively banana-like shape and size. *Ariolimax* is from
the Latin for "slug"; *columbianus* honors the Columbia
River, where these slugs were first studied.
SIZE: Adults to ten inches long, more regularly six inches
COLOR: Body olive to brown with black splotches, some populations vivid yellow
NOTES: The banana slug is the official mascot of the University
of California at Santa Cruz.

WHEN YOU THINK OF A SLUG, what comes to mind? Most of our
images of these shell-less terrestrial relatives of snails are negative.
Slugs are slimy. They ooze through yards and gardens, consuming
tender plant sprouts, flowers, and other delicacies. They are
squishy underfoot. They are poisonous. Even the name has negative connotations: to be a slug is to be lazy, slow, inactive, or idle.

Is there a positive side to slugs? For native species such as the
banana slug, most definitely yes. (Most garden slugs are non-
natives.) Banana slugs are important to the life of the temperate
rain forests of the Pacific coast, from the redwood groves of the
California coast to the Sitka spruce and western hemlock forests
of southeastern Alaska. These detritus feeders crawl across the

forest floor and up tree trunks in search of food: fungi, lichens, algae, plant material of all kinds, animal carcasses, and animal scat. Banana slugs are decomposers, recycling crucial nutrients by digesting plant and animal tissues and enriching the soil with their droppings.

Banana slugs and the giant trees that shade them may actually be interdependent. In an experiment with coast redwood seedlings, researchers discovered that not only did banana slugs avoid eating redwood seedlings, they gave the redwoods a competitive boost by consuming competing plant seedlings. Further, their nitrogen-rich droppings acted as fertilizer, speeding the redwoods' growth. Researchers also think these mollusks aid in disseminating fungi—crucial to trees' survival—throughout temperate rain forests. Trees depend on the rootlike underground threads, or mycorrhizae, of fungi to extend their own root systems. Mycorrhizae form partnerships with tree roots, drawing water and nutrients into the tree and helping the tree resist disease. The fungus, in turn, feeds on the tree's sugary sap. A banana slug crawls up onto a tasty mushroom and eats the succulent tissues, spores and all. The spores pass unharmed through the slug's digestive system, are carried along as it slimes through the forest, then finally are deposited in pats of slug fertilizer. The spores sprout and grow fungal mycorrhizae, which form partnerships with tree root systems. During the rainy fall and winter, the myc orrhizae produce fruiting bodies such as mushrooms, attracting hungry banana slugs.

Slugs are snails that have dispensed with shells. In trading away their spiral homes, slugs free themselves from the need for high-calcium food and save the energy required to lug around the unwieldy shell. But they lose the protective advantage of a shell to retreat into. Instead, slugs coat their bodies with a thick layer of repellent slime or mucus. Not only does the mucus make for a gummy, gaggy mouthful, it is also anesthetic. As my daughter, Molly, discovered years ago when we lived in slug country in western Washington, if you lick a banana slug, your tongue goes numb.

Repulsive as a banana slug may be, an assortment of predators do dine on them. Several species of flightless forest-dwelling beetles consume small slugs; shrews, voles, and moles eat them; salamanders and newts swallow banana slugs almost as large as themselves; garter snakes, foxes, raccoons, porcupines, and crows also consume banana slugs. The Yurok Indians of California's northern coast ate banana slugs when other food was scarce, and American settlers reportedly removed the slime with vinegar and fried banana slugs in batter. (Slugs, after all, are simply escargot without the shell.)

A banana slug's slime is extraordinary stuff. Secreted from a gland under their mantle, the leathery covering on the front end of a slug's body, it serves as a defense, a cushion that protects the slug's soft body from sharp objects, and an adhesive that allows them to travel upside down. Banana slugs can even "rappel" from trees or other heights by spinning a slime cord from the mucus plug at the end of their tail and lowering themselves slowly to the ground.

Perhaps the most bizarre use of their slime, however, is for sex. When banana slugs are in the mood, they advertise for partners by scenting their slime trails with special chemicals. Like snails and sea slugs, banana slugs are hermaphroditic, carrying both male and female organs, but they mate in pairs. The two amorous slugs circle each other and engage in hours of foreplay, licking, biting, and stimulating each other until, mantles tightly pressed together, the long penis of each penetrates the other's genital opening. The pair remains thus for several more hours, then separates—if the two can. Often, the penis of one banana slug becomes stuck, and to free itself, that slug must chew off its own organ. (It later regenerates.)

After a mating ritual that may last twelve hours, the two slugs go their separate ways. Each eventually lays a clutch of thirty or so eggs in a moist spot in the soil. If all goes well, the peppercorn-sized eggs hatch into colorless, inch-long slugs, which ooze across the forest floor in search of food. As they eat and grow, banana slugs contribute their mite to the wet forests that harbor them.

Coast Redwood

Palo colorado
Sequoia sempervirens

Coast Redwood
(sequoia sempervirens)

Our tree-pals
breathing-partners, our
buddies.
How can we treat them like we do?
—Clifford Burke, "Whulge," *Whulj*

RANGE: Along the coast, from extreme southwestern Oregon to central California, from sea level to three thousand feet in elevation

HABITAT: Sandy soils on valley-bottom flats, terraces, or lower slopes

NAME: Coast redwoods grow only within the fog belt along the Pacific coast; the wood of old trees is distinctly rufous red. *Palo colorado*, the Spanish name, means "red bark." *Sequoia* honors the Cherokee Indian Sequoya, inventor of the Cherokee alphabet; *sempervirens*, "evergreen," refers to the tree's foliage.

SIZE: Mature trees reach heights of two hundred to three-hundred-plus feet, trunks up to twenty feet in diameter

COLOR: Bark rufous to brown, wood red to ivory, leaves small, needlelike, and green

NOTES: The world's tallest tree is a 368-foot-tall coast redwood; these trees can live upward of two thousand years.

NOT FAR FROM my former office on the campus of Washington's state capitol is a vacant lot, a wild tangle of blackberry canes and salal shrub sandwiched between a parking lot and a four-lane street. All that remains of the house that once stood there are a set of moss-grown steps, the outline of a cellar hole, and a tree—a huge tree, with a swelling, buttressed trunk some twenty-five feet around and so tall that it far overtops its arboreal neighbors, even with its top snagged off by a winter storm. When I worked nearby, I used to visit the tree often. I'd pick my way through the tangle to its massive base and stand next to it, one hand flat on its thick bark, feeling its life as we both breathed quietly, the great tree and I.

My tree buddy is a coast redwood, planted far north of its native range by some Victorian homeowner with a taste for the exotic. Coast redwoods are the giants in a world of big trees, the temperate rain forests of the northern Pacific coast. These forests, once a solid band stretching from northern California to southeast Alaska, grow so uniformly tall that the record trees for each species rarely stand out among their fellows. Nearly half of the twenty-five tallest species of trees in the world grow here. Not only are these temperate rain forest trees tall, they are old as well. Middle age for them is reckoned in centuries; venerable old age means a millennia or more. These maritime forests are also some of the most productive in the world: while tropical jungles can produce 180 tons of biomass per acre (biomass is the total matter, living and dead, produced by the ecosystem), the coniferous rain forests of the northern Pacific coast can produce between four hundred and fifteen hundred tons per acre! Old-growth coast redwood forests are the most productive of all. An acre of redwood forest accumulates four thousand pounds of wood alone each year.

What makes these forests so phenomenally productive? Rain—lots of it—and a climate kept clement by the moderating influence of the ocean. From the sixty inches of precipitation a year that characterizes the redwood forests to over two hundred inches per year of the forests of the Alaska Panhandle, these are wet woods. Fog drip adds additional precipitation, especially for the redwood forests, where fog may add another foot of moisture each year. There is one hitch to the abundant precipitation: most of it falls in the coldest months of the year, the time when many plants are dormant. The driest part of the year comes during the growing season; in fact, on the southern end of the range where the coast redwoods thrive, months may go by with no rain. Evergreen trees with their waxy, drought-resistant leaves are best suited to these conditions, since they are able to photosynthesize during the rainy season and wait out the droughts.

Coast redwoods are the southernmost species of the temperate rain forests. Although in prehistoric times these giant trees were common across the entire North American continent, they are now confined to the fog belt of the central Pacific coast. Even within this zone, coast redwoods are finicky. They grow inland only in east-west-trending river valleys, where offshore summer breezes blow fog far inland. They are picky about soils as well, thriving only on sandy soils supplied with plenty of nutrients.

Although finicky about growing conditions, these giant trees are no weaklings. Once established, they handily survive summer drought, winter floods, and natural fire—all conditions of their contradictorily rain-rich, drought-plagued environment. During winter's torrential rains, creeks and rivers often flood over their banks, depositing thick layers of sediment where these huge trees grow. The blanket of new soil and nutrients is a bonus for the forest, but often buries the individual trees' roots, cutting off their gas exchange. (Tree roots must be able to breathe.) When debris buries a coast redwood's root layer, the tree simply grows a new layer upward into the new, fertile soil layer. At one site, researchers found fifteen layers of root systems going down twenty-eight feet into the soil for one tree, each corresponding to a new flood over the past thousand years.

Coast redwoods grow bark up to a foot thick as an adaptation to the lightning-caused fires that once swept these forests during summer droughts. Such fires, scientists now believe, cleared out the sometimes crowded forest underlayer, killing young trees and shrubs, and thus reducing the competition to the big redwoods already standing. Fires also burned up some of the downed material on the forest floor, releasing nutrients to promote new growth. Where fire killed an area of larger trees, the resultant opening stimulated the release of seeds from adjacent trees' cones and allowed new redwoods to germinate. A coast redwood can also sprout from tumorlike growths, or burls, at the base of its buttressed trunks. Once thought to be caused by disease or parasites, burls are actually stem buds that sprout new shoots if the trunk is destroyed.

The old saying about not being able to see the forest for the trees is apt for coast redwoods and for the Pacific Coast's temperate rain forests. Although the trees are the most obvious symbol of these forests, what makes the forest—and allows the trees to thrive—are the webs of other living creatures so intricate that it is almost impossible to separate all the strands and parse out all of the relationships. For example, take a species of lichen that grows high up in the canopy of coast redwoods and other trees. The lichen harvests nitrogen out of the air and stores it in its tissues. When a lichen falls or is blown out of the canopy and lands on the forest floor, grazers such as banana slugs and red-backed voles consume it. Their droppings add the lichen's nitrogen to the soil, nurturing the trees that harbored the lichen.

When a coast redwood dies, the snag may stand for two hundred years, providing homes for a whole host of animals and plants—including some sixty species of birds and mammals—that need standing dead trees. When the giant finally falls, its decaying trunk lies on the forest floor for centuries, housing and feeding more than 130 species of vertebrates, from salamanders to bats, and uncounted species of invertebrates and plants, from banana slugs to mosses. The fallen tree trunk soaks up and stores water like a giant sponge, releasing it slowly to wet the soil in the dry months. Redwood trunks that fall across streams slow and aerate the water and trap sediment, maintaining spawning habitat for salmon and oceangoing trout. They house and feed aquatic insects and other lives, which themselves feed a host of other creatures: salamanders, frogs, salmon, trout, otters, raccoons, dippers, and bears.

Coast redwoods and the other giant trees of the temperate rain forests nurture humans too. As the poet Clifford Burke points out, they are our "breathing-buddies." In the process of making food from sunlight, trees, like most plants, pull in carbon dioxide and exhale oxygen as a waste product. Humans, of course, live on oxygen; we exhale carbon dioxide. By their respiration, the temperate rain forests add literally tons of oxygen to the atmosphere, making life on this planet possible for humans.

On a recent visit to Olympia, Washington, I pressed my hand to the furrowed trunk of the coast redwood in the vacant lot, and imagined that our breathing—mine and the great tree's—synchronized. As I breathed out my unwanted carbon dioxide, the great tree breathed in. As it exhaled life-giving oxygen, I inhaled. As I breathed, I felt the connection that binds humans and wild lives everywhere: it takes us all to make the miracle that is life on earth.

Recommended Readings & Places to Visit

HERE ARE MY SUGGESTIONS on resources for learning more about these Pacific Coast lives, plus places to go to see them. This is not an exhaustive list; rather, these are some of my favorite books, magazines, and web sites. Nor are my recommendations of where to go the only possibilities, just the places I prefer.

SPRING

Eelgrass: The quote is from Gary Snyder's eloquent and thought-provoking meditation on being human, *The Practice of the Wild* (Farrar, Straus & Giroux, 1990). Nontechnical sources on eelgrass are difficult to find; however, Stewart Schultz's *The Northwest Coast* (Timber Press, 1990) and *Seashore Life of the Northern Pacific Coast* (Eugene N. Kozloff, Univ. of Washington Press, 1993) are both useful. My favorite place to see eelgrass is at Padilla Bay National Estuarine Reserve, near Mount Vernon, Washington. Visit at low tide in late spring or summer to see the verdant tangle of eelgrass, in fall or winter to see the incredible flocks of waterfowl.

Rough-skinned Newt: The quote is from *Riverwalking: Reflections on Moving Water* (Lyons & Burford, 1995), Kathleen Dean Moore's meditation on her relationship with nature. One chapter is devoted to the story of these amazing newts. Another useful reference is *Seasonal Guide to the Natural Year: Oregon, Washington, British Columbia* by James Luther Davis (Fulcrum Publishing, 1996). My favorite place to see rough-skinned newts is the McClane Creek Nature Trail in Capitol Forest, west of Olympia, Washington.

California Poppy: Karen B. Nilsson's *A Wildflower by Any Other Name* (Yosemite Association, 1994) is the source of the quote and a wonderful introduction to the personalities behind plants' scientific names. Although long out of print, Charles Francis Saunders's *Western Wildflowers and Their Stories* (Doubleday Duran, 1933) has interesting information on California poppies. To see California poppy displays, visit the Antelope Valley Poppy Reserve (805-724-1180), near Lancaster, north of Los Angeles, or the Bear Valley Road between Williams and Willits in northern California, or call the Theodore Payne Foundation (818-768-3533) for information on wildflowers in southern California.

Black Oystercatcher: Kenn Kaufman's delightful and informative *Lives of North American Birds* (Houghton Mifflin, 1996) is the source of the quote and also a good reference. For more, try *The Audubon Society Encyclopedia of North American Birds,* by John K. Terres (Alfred A. Knopf, 1980). My favorite places to look for black oystercatchers are at Pescadero Beach State Park on the San Francisco Peninsula or on any rocky shore in the San Juan Islands of Washington.

Giant Pacific Octopus: John Steinbeck's classic *Cannery Row* (Viking Press, 1945) is the source of the quote. A fascinating, if dated, reference is Jacques-Yves Cousteau and Philippe Diolé's book, *Octopus and Squid: The Soft Intelligence* (Doubleday & Co., 1975). Also try Edward F. Ricketts, et al., *Between Pacific Tides* (Stanford Univ. Press, fifth edition, 1985). Unless you are an experienced scuba diver, the best places to see these enormous creatures are aquariums, such as the Oregon Coast Aquarium (541-867-4931), near Newport, Oregon.

California Grunion: Barbara Kingsolver's beautifully written, funny, and poignant book of essays, *High Tide in Tucson* (Harper

Perennial, 1995), is the source of the quote. Allan A. Schoenherr's *A Natural History of California* (Univ. of California Press, 1992) is a good reference on these unusual beach-spawning fish. The Cabrillo Marine Aquarium (310-548-7562), in San Pedro, south of Los Angeles, has grunion programs and spawning information. Nearby Cabrillo Beach is a great place to watch grunion runs.

Red Abalone: Edward F. Ricketts, et al., *Between Pacific Tides*, is the source of the quote and also an excellent reference on red abalone (and any other intertidal life of the Pacific Coast). If you're a diver, the best place to see these big mollusks is in the waters off the Channel Islands National Park. If you don't dive, your best hope of seeing red abalones is in a coastal aquarium, such as the Stephen Birch Aquarium Museum (619-534-3474) at the Scripps Institute of Oceanography in La Jolla, California.

Blueblossom: The quote is from Peter Fish's article "Chaparral" in *Sunset* magazine, April 1994. Donald Culross Peattie's charmingly written *A Natural History of Western Trees* (Houghton Mifflin, reissued 1991) and Allan Schoenherr's *A Natural History of California*, are good references on California lilac. My favorite place to see and smell these characteristic chaparral shrubs in bloom is along the Big Basin Road in Santa Cruz County. Also try the Rancho Santa Ana Botanical Garden (909-625-8767), Claremont, longtime breeders of these natives, for a dazzling show.

Pacific Madrone: The quote is from David Rains Wallace's marvelous book about the mountains where Oregon and California meet, *The Klamath Knot* (Sierra Club Books, 1983). Look for more about madrone in *A Natural History of Western Trees* and *A Natural History of California*. My favorite place to see madrones (though they grow much bigger farther south) is along Hood

Canal in Washington's Puget Sound, where they writhe out of the shoreline rocks like rufous snakes.

White Sturgeon: Elliot Coues's classic *The History of the Lewis and Clark Expedition* (Dover Publications reprint, Vol. II) is the source of the quote. Popular information about white sturgeon is hard to come by. The *White Sturgeon Management Framework Plan* (Pacific States Marine Fisheries Commission, 1992) is a very readable technical publication. Seeing these giant bottom-dwelling fish isn't easy. Try the City of Vancouver Washington's Water Resources Education Center (360-696-8478) on the Columbia River, or look for captive white sturgeon in U.S. Army Corps of Engineers' ponds at the Dalles Dam.

SUMMER

Southern Sea Otter: One of my favorite books about the Pacific Coast, Page Stegner and Frans Lanting's *Islands of the West: From Baja to Vancouver* (Sierra Club Books, 1985), is the source of the quote. Gary Turbak's *Survivors in the Shadows* (Northland Press, 1993) is a first-rate source of information, and Edwin Way Teale's classic *Autumn Across America* (Dodd, Mead & Co., 1956) gives a fascinating first-person account of watching sea otters. My favorite place to watch these "aquabats" is from the pullouts along Highway One from Carmel south to San Simeon, along Big Sur. If you don't see otters, the scenery will make up for it! Or visit the Monterey Bay Aquarium (408-648-4800) to watch sea otters gambol in their indoor tank.

Cabezon: The Ernest Hemingway quote comes from the Quotations Volume in Microsoft Bookself 1996. Information about cabezon is scarce in popular literature. Look for cabezon in Judith Connor and Charles Baxter's *Kelp Forests* (Monterey Bay

Aquarium, 1989) and in *National Audubon Society Field Guide to North American Fishes, Whales & Dolphins* (Alfred A. Knopf, 1997). Unless you are an accomplished diver, the easiest way to see these remarkable looking fish is at an aquarium such as the brand-new Long Beach Aquarium of the Pacific (562-590-3100) in Long Beach, California.

Cobra Lily: James Luther Davis's *A Seasonal Guide to the Natural Year: Oregon, Washington, British Columbia* is the source of the quote and also a good source of information on these odd plants. Also try Eugene Kozloff's *Plants and Animals of the Pacific Northwest* (Univ. of Washington Press, 1976). The best place to see cobra lilies in yellow-green crowds is at the state of Oregon's Darlingtonia Wayside, north of Florence on Highway 101.

Xerces Blue Butterfly: John Cody is quoted in an exhibit at the Tijuana River National Estuarine Research Reserve Visitor Center. Since the Xerces blue is extinct, not much information is available on their lives, nor can you see them except in study collections. You can see yellow bush lupine, however, on sand dunes and sandy cliffs up and down the coast. My favorite place to see and smell these fragrant lupines is at the Nature Conservancy's Guadalupe-Nipomo Dunes Preserve (805-545-9925), a magical patch of dunes accessible by a boardwalk across Oso Flaco ("Skinny Bear") Lake.

Bat Ray: Edward O. Wilson's fascinating autobiography, *Naturalist* (Warner Books, 1994), is the source of the quote. Look up bat rays in *Between Pacific Tides* and *National Audubon Society Field Guide to North American Fishes, Whales & Dolphins*. My favorite place to see bat rays, the Monterey Bay Aquarium (408-648-4800), is also one of the best sources of information on these amazing shark relatives.

Light-footed Clapper Rail: Sharman Apt Russell's thought-provoking book *Kill the Cowboy: A Battle of Mythology in the New West* (Addison-Wesley, 1993) is the source of the quote. Look in Peter Steinhart's *California's Wild Heritage* (Sierra Club Books, 1990) and *A Natural History of California* for more information. Seeing a light-footed clapper rail is not an easy task; you are more likely to hear these secretive birds. Try Upper Newport Bay Ecological Preserve (714-640-6746), Newport Beach, California, or the Tijuana River National Estuarine Research Reserve (619-575-3613), Imperial Beach.

Orca: *Nature and Other Mothers: Personal Stories of Women and the Body of Earth* (Fawcett Columbine, 1992), by Brenda Peterson, is the source of the quote and one of my favorite books. The American Cetacean Society's *Field Guide to the Orca* (Sasquatch Books, 1990), by David G. Gordon and Chuck Flaherty, is a thorough orca reference. The best place to see orcas in summer is Johnstone Strait, at the north end of Vancouver Island, British Columbia. (Take a whale-watching cruise; the shoreline is closed to protect the orcas.) Or tune in to ORCA FM (CJKW 88.5) in the Vancouver, Canada, area.

Geoduck Clam: The Evergreen State College in Olympia, Washington, has adopted the geoduck as their official mascot. Their motto is the source of the quote. Popular information on geoducks is scattered; try *Between Pacific Tides* or call the Washington State Department of Natural Resources (360-902-1000) for their publications. Look for geoducks' large spouts as the tide goes out on sandy mudflats, or look for these giant clams on ice at fish markets, including Seattle's Pike Street Market.

Giant Green Anemone: Edwin Way Teale's natural history travelogue, *Autumn Across America* (Dodd, Mead & Co., 1956), is the source of the quote. *Between Pacific Tides* and *The Seashore Life of Oregon, Washington and British Columbia* are both solid references. The tide pools at Yaquina Head Outstanding Natural Area (541-574-3100), north of Newport, Oregon, are good places to look for these anemones and a host of other intertidal life. (Yaquina Head is truly outstanding, both scenically and biologically. It is also the only place on the Pacific coast that I know of with wheelchair-accessible tide pools.)

Marbled Murrelet: Allan A. Schoenherr's *A Natural History of California* is the source of the quote. Kenn Kaufman's *Lives of North American Birds* is an informative marbled murrelet reference. The discussion of alcid and penguin evolution comes from *The Birder's Handbook,* by Paul R. Ehrlich, David S. Dobkin, and Darryl Wheye (Simon & Schuster, 1988). In winter, look for marbled murrelets in bays and inlets, especially Puget Sound. In summer, try Big Basin Redwoods State Park near Santa Cruz, California. For underwater views of alcids' incredible swimming ability, visit the Seattle Aquarium (206-386-4320).

FALL

Harford's Greedy Isopod: Gertrude Ederle was quoted in a story in the *New York Post* (September 5, 1956), thirty years after becoming the first woman to swim the English Channel. Ricketts, et al., *Between Pacific Tides,* is a useful reference on these odd marine scavengers. Look for Harford's greedy isopods at low tide under rocks on any sandy sea bottom.

California Least Tern: Peter Steinhart's beautifully written look at California's threatened and endangered species, *California's Wild Heritage,* is the source of the quote and also a good reference. Also look for "A Turn for the Better: California's Least Tern," a pamphlet published by the Don Edwards San Francisco Bay National Wildlife Refuge. My favorite place to look for California least terns is Bolsa Chica, a restored marsh just off Highway One in Huntington Beach, California.

Eccentric Sand Dollar: Delta Willis's look at nature's engineering, *The Sand Dollar and the Slide Rule* (Addison-Wesley, 1995), is the source of the quote. *Between Pacific Tides* and Donald J. Zinn's *Handbook for Beach Strollers* (Univ. of Rhode Island Marine Bulletin No. 12, 1973) are both excellent sources of information on these unusual creatures. You can find sand dollar shells on any sandy beach after fall or winter storms. Or visit the Monterey Bay Aquarium (408-648-4800) to see a fascinating exhibit of a sand dollar colony.

Pickleweed: Charles Francis Saunders's book, *Western Wildflowers and Their Stories,* is the source of the quote. *Seashore Life of the Northern Pacific Coast* and *A Natural History of California* are good sources of information on pickleweed. My favorite place to see masses of pickleweed is around San Francisco Bay, especially at Don Edwards San Francisco Bay National Wildlife Refuge (510-792-4275).

Giant Acorn Barnacle: The quote comes from Rachel Carson's classic *The Edge of the Sea* (Houghton Mifflin Co., reissued 1983). *Between Pacific Tides* is a good source of more information about these huge barnacles. Look for giant acorn barnacles below the high-tide line on rocks and pilings. If you can, watch them as the tide comes up to see their tightly closed, seemingly dead shells come alive.

Brown Pelican: Dixon Lanier Merritt's 1910 limerick is quoted in *The Seasonal Guide to the Natural Year: Southern California and Baja California* (Fulcrum Publishing, 1997), by Judy Wade. For more on brown pelicans, try Kenn Kaufman's *The Lives of North American Birds* and *The Audubon Society Encyclopedia of North American Birds*. For more on DDT and its effect on pelicans, read *Islands of the West*. My favorite place to watch pelicans fly by and dive into the waves is from the bluffs at Torrey Pines State Park in La Jolla, California.

Diatoms: Lewis Thomas's thoughtful meditation on the nature of life, *Lives of a Cell: Notes of a Biology Watcher* (Viking Penguin, 1987), is the source of the quote. Because diatoms are minute and not easily seen, they are not much discussed in popular literature. Rachel Carson's *The Edge of the Sea* and *Seashore Life of the Northern Pacific Coast* are good references. You can't see individual diatoms except under a microscope. Look for exhibits on these fascinating algae and their exquisitely detailed crystalline boxes in coastal museums or aquariums.

Moon Jellyfish: The quote comes from *Between Pacific Tides,* also a good source of information on moon jellyfish and their unusual lives. *A Guide to the World of Jellyfish* (Monterey Bay Aquarium Foundation, 1992) is a thorough introduction to jellies, especially for children. My favorite place to see jellies indoors is at the Long Beach Aquarium (562-590-3100), where a variety of these creatures pulsate with breathtaking beauty in special tanks. For a very different view of jellies, walk a beach after a fall storm and look for jellies in the tide rows, the lines of debris washed up on the beach.

Harbor Seal: *Marine Birds and Mammals of Puget Sound,* by Tony Angell and Kenneth C. Balcomb III (Univ. of Washington Press, 1982), is the source of the quote and a good source of information on harbor seals, as is *A Natural History of California.* I've had my most memorable encounters with harbor seals while sea kayaking, both in Puget Sound and in Bandon Estuary, near

Bandon, Oregon. Look for harbor seal rookeries on quiet beaches all along the Pacific coast.

Chum Salmon: Philip Drucker is quoted in *Mountain in the Clouds* (Simon & Schuster, 1982), Bruce Brown's eloquent and tragic history of the decline of Pacific Northwest salmon. Goldstream Provincial Park, northwest of Victoria on Vancouver Island, still boasts spectacular chum runs in the Goldstream River. Or visit the Skagit River Bald Eagle Natural Area, between Concrete and Marblemont, Washington, to watch hundreds of bald eagles congregate to feed on spawned-out chums.

WINTER

Giant Bladder Kelp: *The Pacific Shore: Meeting Place of Man and Nature* (E. P. Dutton, 1974), by Dennis Brokaw and Wesley Marx, is the source of the quote. A good kelp reference is *Kelp Forests,* by Judith Connor and Charles Baxter (Monterey Bay Aquarium, 1989). Walk any Pacific Coast beach after a winter storm, and you're bound to find pieces of giant bladder kelp or the bare, hoselike stipe of bull kelp. The best way to know kelp beds is to take a dive trip into a shadowy undersea jungle off one of the islands in the Channel Islands National Park (805-658-5730). Or visit the fantastic indoor giant kelp forest exhibit at the Monterey Bay Aquarium (408-648-4800).

Sanderling: The quote comes from "Words to Live By," from *This Week* magazine, May 25, 1952, and is also quoted in *Rachel Carson: Witness to Nature* (Henry Holt and Co., 1997), by Linda Lear. The *Birder's Handbook,* by Paul R. Ehrlich, David S. Dobkin, and Darryl Wheye, is an excellent reference on sanderlings and bird migration. *Lives of North American Birds,* by Kenn Kaufman, is another useful source of information about these gray ghosts.

Look for sanderlings on any sandy Pacific Coast beach in winter. My favorite place to watch these small sandpipers is the broad beach at Ocean Shores, Washington.

Spanish Shawl: John Steinbeck's *Cannery Row,* with its wonderful evocations of the marine life in and around Monterey, California, is the source of the quote. *Handbook for Beach Strollers* by Donald J. Zinn is a good resource on nudibranchs in general, as is *Seashore Life of the Northern Pacific Coast,* which includes gorgeous color photos of many species. Look for the vivid colors of Spanish shawls around pilings and in tide pools all along the Pacific coast, especially in central and southern California.

Island Fox: Dwight Holing's introduction to California in *The Smithsonian Guides to Natural America: The Far West* (Smithsonian Books, 1996) is the source of the quote. *A Natural History of California* tells the story of how these small foxes came to the Channel Islands; Gary Turbak's *Survivors in the Shadows* is a fine source of information about their lives. To see these smallest of North American foxes requires a trip to one of the Channel Islands. Or visit the Channel Islands National Park Visitor Center (805-658-5730) in Ventura, California, where the displays of endemic island flora and fauna include two stuffed island foxes.

Monarch Butterfly: The quote is the text of the original city ordinance protecting monarchs in Pacific Grove, California. The Xerces Society (503-232-6639) publishes information on monarchs, including "The Monarch Habitat Handbook." For kids, check out Monarch Watch's web site (www.MonarchWatch.org). For a sense of the poetry of these insects' lives, read Alison Deming's lyrical and thoughtful examination of monarchs and the nature of intelligence, *The Monarchs* (Louisiana State Univ. Press, 1997). The classic place to see roosting monarchs between October and March is in Pacific Grove, California, but larger numbers may be seen at Natural Bridges State Park (408-423-4609) across Monterey Bay in Santa Cruz.

Gray Whale: Diane Ackerman's essay collection, *The Moon by Whale Light* (Vintage Books, 1992), is the source of the quote and a fascinating look at whales and whale research. *The Oceanic Society Field Guide to the Gray Whale* (Sasquatch Books, 1989) is a succinct and useful resource to these marvelous mammals. Any prominent bluff or jetty on the Pacific coast offers great opportunities to watch gray whales in migration. For a closer view, take a trip to San Ignacio or Scammon's Lagoon, Baja California, in February or March. Dana Point, in southern California's Orange County, throws a whalefest each February (1-800-290-DANA) and, at the opposite end of the coast, Tofino and Ucluelet, Vancouver Island, host the Pacific Rim Whale Festival (604-725-3414) in March. The Whale Museum (360-378-4710) in Friday Harbor, San Juan Islands, offers a fascinating look at whales in life and art.

Western Gull: Judy Wade's *Seasonal Guide to the Natural Year: Southern California and Baja California* is the source of the quote. Kenn Kaufman's *Lives of North American Birds* is a useful resource on western gulls; the discussion of super-species comes from *The Birder's Handbook*. Look for western gulls anywhere along the Pacific coast. The largest nesting colony, some 35,000 birds, is on the Farallon Islands, northwest of San Francisco.

Banana Slug: The John Muir quote comes from Alice Bryant Harper's fascinating and informative *The Banana Slug* (Bay Leaves Press, 1993), which is also the best single source of information on these amazing mollusks. The Xerces Society's journal, *Wings* (503-232-6639), includes a variety of articles on slugs and other temperate rain forest invertebrates. Look for banana slugs on rainy fall and winter days (100 percent humidity is perfect weather for these creatures!) in moist forests, especially old-growth, anywhere from central California north.

Coast Redwood: Clifford Burke's chapbook, *Whulj* (Tanagram, 1991), is the source of the quote, and a beautiful evocation of life on Puget Sound. Unlike some of the lives profiled in this book, information on coast redwoods abounds. Look in *A Natural History of California* and Joan Dunning and Doug Thron's *From the Redwood Forest* (Chelsea Green, 1998), as well as in Donald Culross Peattie's *A Natural History of Western Trees*. My favorite place to see coast redwood forests at their most magnificent is the Avenue of the Giants in Humboldt Redwoods State Park (707-946-2409), south of Eureka, California. Go on a foggy day, put your hand on the trunk of one of these giants, stand still, and just breathe.